May The Lord Bless
All That You Do.

RESTORING TRUE IDENTITY

Encounter the Ups and Downs in the Life of a Disciple

CHRIS BROOKS

WESTBOW
PRESS®
A DIVISION OF THOMAS NELSON
& ZONDERVAN

WestBow Press books may be ordered through booksellers or by contacting:

WestBow Press
A Division of Thomas Nelson & Zondervan
1663 Liberty Drive
Bloomington, IN 47403
www.westbowpress.com
1 (866) 928-1240

ISBN: 978-1-9736-8255-4 (sc)
ISBN: 978-1-9736-8256-1 (hc)
ISBN: 978-1-9736-8257-8 (e)\

Library of Congress Control Number: 2019920903

Print information available on the last page.

WestBow Press rev. date: 01/08/2020

In Chris Brooks' new book, RESTORING TRUE IDENTITY, he courageously takes us on a very personal journey into his own life and ministry. His is a story of humility, honesty, and a refreshing dose of pure transparency — all qualities that cause his ministry to be one of genuine effectiveness.

In this book, Chris says, "Your yes is what the Lord is patiently waiting for." I'm so thankful that Chris said "Yes" when given the instruction to write this book, and I believe you, too, will be grateful for the YES as you read and receive revelation on the subject of restoring true identity.

What I especially appreciate about this book is the obvious time Chris has invested in prayer, in the Word, and in his personal study — all of which seamlessly come together in a book that can forever change your life.

I encourage you to read this book; to hear the heartbeat of the Father on its pages; and in the end, allow Jesus to Restore True Identity in your very own life.

Dean Sikes
Founder - YouMatter
Dean Sikes Ministries

In Restoring True Identity, Chris Brooks blends his transparent journey with powerful revelation and scriptural application to write a profound testimony of hope for those in the Body of Christ who need encouragement and strength. The testimony of Jesus is the Spirit of prophecy. Chris' testimony of all that The Lord has done for him, is a prophetic declaration what God is going to do in your life. Be strengthened! This book will bring you hope!

Kevin Wallace
Senior Pastor Redemption to the Nations
Chattanooga, Tn.

Chris's work in RESTORING TRUE IDENTITY is a blend of personal testimony and Biblical definitions that highlight the Christian experience. It's relaxed but at the same time cuts into Christian purpose precisely. Christian works like these touch all of us with life experiences we all can relate to but at the same time brings focus on maturity. This work coming from the heart of an evangelist replenishes our spirits with fresh energy. It will take the reader in and out, under and over, using the Gospel to point the way to Christian conquest. I especially like the way Chris uses the disciples and Christ interplay revealing the core message.

I highly recommend this work because there is excitement, setbacks, challenges, and victories x-rayed through the Word of God.

Michael Lindon

Thank You

To my loving wife Davi, you are the most
incredible woman of God I know.
For the past few years of writing this book your encouragement
and words of affirmation have propelled me to accomplish
something I never thought I would have the ability to complete.

To my Daughter Faith. I cannot express enough or put
into words as a father how proud I am of you. Your
identity in Christ has never wavered! I have watched you
stand against adversity and come out like a champ!
Daddy loves you.

To Danial a true son in the Faith. Without you this
would not have happened! All the work you put into
this project, your tireless help and dedication is priceless.
You and Lindsay are treasures to Davi and I. We Declare
and Decree 1000-fold blessing into your lives!

To My Spiritual Father Michael Linden. When Holy
Spirit spoke to you that Friday night at the football game
and said that you would not be wasting your time with
me; I am so glad that You said Yes! During the darkest
time in my life I know for a fact that the Lord sent you to
me! You have shown me what a true Father in the Faith
looks like. I am forever grateful to have you in my life.

To Dean Sikes my friend. I have to say that from the day I met you in a cafe downtown Chattanooga and you Prophesied over Davi and I, right then I knew that you were someone I wanted to glen from. Not many friends will tell you how the cow eats the cabbage, but you did! Thank you for being real to Davi and I, holding nothing back.

To Pastor Kevin Wallace. When I read my Bible and it mentions the Pastor, I see you. You are a Pastor to the Nations and a voice of redemption not just to Chattanooga, but to the world. Davi and I honor you as our Pastor, enjoy you as our friend and love you as our brother in Christ!

To Mama Karen. You have always been a voice of fire into my life since 2005. From the night we met at the Ramp, I have never forgotten that precious encounter. You have taught Davi and I how to live in our God given identity. You pulled the revivalist out of me, stretched me to believe bigger, trust with reckless abandonment, command the Word of the Lord to come and shake all that can be shaken. To say the least, I found out who I really was called by God to be under your tutelage and covering. We love you Mama K, and always will.

To the CBM Board members, we thank each of you for all your support, prayers, and friendship. Getting to do life with each of you is a true honor.

To my Lord and Savior! Thank you for never giving up on that hard headed boy from East Texas. I have grown to know you as a friend, brother, Father, and my King! When I thought I was a nobody, you called me your own. When I thought I was not good enough, you came to live in me and make up for my imperfections. When I said I can't, you said yes you can! When I tried to run from my calling, leave it all behind, you taught me these words, Thy Will Be Done! I can never thank you, give to you, our bless you with my lips enough to add up what you have done for me! But I am going to try my best. Love ya, talk to ya later

Contents

Foreward

"Who do you say that I am?"

The question thunders from the mouth of God into the heart of every person who has ever been given the gift of life. He demands a response.

Two thousand years ago, twelve men found themselves walking the dry dusty roads of the Galilean hillsides with a Man whose voice had awakened in them the hope of revealed purpose. Hidden in each conversation with this unusual Man, there seemed to be messages coming from another world that spoke to the questions inside them—Who am I? Where did I come from? Where am I going? Is there something more to live for?

These wide-eyed men stood in awe as they listened to Him speak. His claims were bold and audacious. He called God His Father and claimed to have preexisted with Him before the world was created. He declared Himself to be the ONLY way to God, the ONLY truth to be found, and the ONLY source of life. He claimed to be able to forgive sins and give satisfying bread to the hungry and living water to the thirsty.

The Twelve watched in amazement as He demonstrated a power that healed the broken, delivered the captive, stilled storms, and sent demons fleeing.

On this particular day, He began a conversation that would reveal to them whether or not they were yet seeing the purpose behind His intentional call and invitation to "follow Him." He began by asking a broad question, "Who do men say that I am?" Unaware that the question was not because He didn't already know, they attempted to answer, "Some say you are John the Baptist. Some say you're Elijah. Some say you're one of the prophets."

With a heavy sigh and longing heart, He looked deep into their searching souls and asked the greater question, "But who do you say that I am?"

As the words penetrated their most profound questions, Peter's response erupted like an exploding geyser, "I say you are the Christ! The Son of the Living God!!"

Jesus whirled around to face him, with fire in His eyes, He replied, "Flesh and blood did not reveal this to you, but my Father which is in heaven! And I say to you that you are Peter and upon the rock, I will build my church and the very gates of hell will not prevail against it! I will give unto you the keys of the Kingdom of heaven. Whatever you bind on earth shall be bound in heaven and whatever you loose on earth shall be loosed in heaven!"

To each generation since Adam, He has called out, "Who do men say that I am?" Our answer sounds eerily similar to the disciples response, "Some say you're just a historical figure. some say you're a prophet. and some say you don't exist. But once again He leans in to each of our hearts and asks the question, "Who do YOU say that I am?"

In this book, like Jesus with the disciples, Chris Brooks invites us to join him on a journey to find the answer to that question and to the questions that have plagued the emptiness of our soul— Who am I? Where did I come from? Where am I going? Is there something more to live for?

As you journey with Chris through these pages, you will come to understand that contained inside the answer to "Who do YOU say that I am?" is the very essence of who you are.

Karen Wheaton
Singer, Worship Leader, Minister, The Ramp
Hamilton, Alabama

One

The Great Encounter

I was sitting in a hanger in Fort Benning, Georgia, gearing up to make my first airborne paratrooper jump along with a couple hundred other nervous soldiers. Now, this was a day I will never forget. I had already completed ground week; during which we had been taught to throw ourselves onto the ground without inflicting any bodily harm. We had also learned to perform a perfect PLF, which is the acronym for prepare, land, and fall.

This had been an exhausting week of "Do it again!" "You fell wrong!" "You missed one of your five points of contact!" (These include the balls of the feet, calves, thigh, buttocks, and push-up muscle.) Come to find out, in real life situations, you only hit three points—feet, butt, and head. Yes, it hurts!

The second week of training was tower week. That was the week we were taught how to exit the aircraft. You don't actually jump out; instead, you just walk out or sometimes run. We practiced again and again, day after day, for a straight week! We'd be hanging in a harness exiting a mock up aircraft while screaming, "One thousand! Two thousand! Three thousand! Four thousand! Opening shock! Check canopy!" We had made it to jump week!

Unfortunately for us, it rained horribly for the first four days of the week. So, what would have been a week of jumping once a day, totaling five jumps, was now going to be three jumps on Friday and two jumps on Saturday. As we waddled our way to the C141—the one we would be walking out of—everything began to become real. The smell of the jet fuel, the sound of the aircraft, and of course the look in everyone's eye—it was all priceless.

As we separated to sit down in our chalks, the groups that would exit the aircraft together, I found myself close to the end of chalk one. That was a good thing! I wouldn't have to go first; all I'd have to do was follow the guy in front of me out the door. Simple. We got the commands from the jumpmaster to stand up. "Hook Up! Check equipment! Sound off for equipment check! All okay, jumpmaster!"

The doors opened, and we couldn't believe how loud it was in that aircraft. "One minute! Thirty seconds! *Go!*" Then, just like that, we walked out the door of a perfectly good airplane. I handed my static line off to the jumpmaster, and all of a sudden, I was on my back on the floor of the plane looking at the ceiling. What happened!

Sergeant Black Hat, which is what we called the instructors, picked me up and said, "Red means stop!" It had taken the guys in front of me longer to exit than anticipated, so when it was time for me to exit, the pilot had turned on the red light. This was a good thing because, if that had not occurred, I would've missed the drop zone! So now I was standing in the door watching the ground go by!

I was no longer in the same pack, and I was now going to be the first one to jump out of the plane. We went through all the checks again. This time I was told to stand in the doorway! Looking at the horizon as I had been taught, waiting for those anticipated words, I felt a slap on the rear and a loud voice saying, *"Go!"* As my body exited the aircraft, my mind was still inside the plane yelling, *What are you doing!*

What happened to me next still is embedded in my memory to this day. Every image of this jump came to me frame by frame. It was as if my mind could not catch up to what was happening. I first saw the ground and my feet. Next, I saw my feet and the guy exiting the aircraft behind me. Then I saw the ground, my feet, and the canopy above my head.

This next part demonstrates that the military needs to come up with some other way of communicating to a couple hundred troopers in the air. The instructors were on the ground with megaphones yelling, "Slip left, slip right. Not you, dummy. I'm talking to you. Not you! *You!*" Confused and disoriented, I decided to just watch out for everyone else. Here I was falling out of the sky, watching for the horizon and preparing to perform a PLF. Then, all of a sudden—*boom!*—I was on the ground like a sack of potatoes. The ever-anticipated ground had come upon me—something I had not expected at quite that moment. What an encounter!

Dictionary.com describes the word *encounter* as follows:

"to come upon or meet with, especially unexpectedly." Not all encounters come with difficulties or oppositions.

I can remember the day I met my wife, Davi. It was in the summer of 1999, and probably to most people's surprise, we did not meet in church, but in a bar in Shreveport, Louisiana. Davi's sister, Wanda, invited us to come to church with their family one Sunday morning. We agreed to go as long as we could sit in the back and leave as soon as they asked people to come forward and cry. I grew up in the Baptist Church, so I knew how this stuff worked.

Although I was not ready for the First Assembly of God in Shreveport, I can remember sitting, shaking and trembling all the way down to my bones. I turned to Davi and said, "If this guy doesn't hurry up and give the altar call, I am going to explode." As soon as the pastor finished preaching, he gave an altar call for repentance. I shot out of the pew like someone had attached me to a rocket ship!

I ran down to the altar and slid face first into the bottom step. Today as I remember, I can just see Jesus in heaven looking down on me, throwing His arms outstretched, and shouting, "Safe!" The next thing I knew, a man put his hand on my back and began to speak into my ear. He told me that God had been waiting for me to get to this moment in my life. I'll never forget what Stan did for me that day, and the year to follow, by speaking into my life and checking in on me every week. Now that's a Christian!

He led me through a simple prayer that started me on my journey with Christ. It was an invitation to have a supernatural *encounter* with a man named Jesus. This was the beginning of my new journey, my new life.

So there was that step I had been looking for.

Today, as we read Luke 5:1–11, we will witness four fishermen as they have an encounter with Jesus. We are going to be paying close attention to the encounter between Jesus and Simon, an encounter that will set Simon on the journey of a lifetime.

> So it was, as the multitude pressed about Him to hear the word of God, that He stood by the Lake of Gennesaret, and saw two boats standing by the lake; but the fishermen had gone from them and were washing their nets. Then He got into one of the boats, which was Simon's, and asked him to put out a little from the land. And He sat down and taught the multitudes from the boat. When He had stopped speaking, He said to Simon, "Launch out into the deep and let down your nets for a catch." But Simon answered and said to Him, "Master, we have toiled all night and caught nothing; nevertheless at Your word I will let down the net." And when they had done this, they caught a great number of fish, and their net was breaking. So they signaled to their partners in the other boat to come and help them. And they came and filled both the boats, so that they began to sink. When Simon Peter saw it, he fell down at Jesus' knees, saying, "Depart from me, for I am a sinful man, O Lord!" For he and all

who were with him were astonished at the catch of fish which they had taken; and so also were James and John, the sons of Zebedee, who were partners with Simon. And Jesus said to Simon, "Do not be afraid. From now on you will catch men." So when they had brought their boats to land, they forsook all and followed Him. (Luke 5:1–11)

Watch closely how Jesus taught the crowd on the shore in the shallow waters. The shallow shore is where most people live their lives. Sure, they show up to Sunday service and listen to the pastor. But they can't tell you what the sermon title was or even the scripture reference. This shallow church function is what Jesus declared as the Loveless Church in Revelation 3:14–16: "These things says the Amen, the Faithful and True Witness, the Beginning of the creation of God: 'I know your works, that you are neither cold nor hot. I could wish you were cold or hot. So then, because you are lukewarm, and neither cold nor hot, I will vomit you out of My mouth.'"

In order to dare to unveil the mysteries of heaven and see God for who He really is, we are going to have to push out into the deep waters. As we read in Psalm 42:7, "Deep calls unto deep at the noise of Your waterfalls; All Your waves and billows have gone over me."

Jesus invited Simon for an encounter into the deep waters. Only deep things can call unto deep things. Our natural way of thinking will have to be left on the shore in order for us to venture into the deep callings of God. Why do I say natural thinking? I am glad you asked. It is because the natural thinking process of Simon is no different than, let's say for clarification, the thinking process in-the-flesh—flesh persons as opposed to spirit persons.

Here we have professional fishermen who have worked hard all night long at the very profession that brings them income. They didn't know if Jesus had any fishing experience. All they knew was the vast knowledge that was coming from His teaching. Now, they had a choice to listen to what Jesus was telling them and push out into the deep waters for a catch.

Most in-the-flesh humans would rise up and say, "Thanks, but no thanks. I'm tired. We have fished all night and caught nothing. I'm going home!" This is where your journey as a Christian must take a newfound leap of faith so that you can see deep things come to pass. Simon did try his best to explain their nightly dilemma, but then quickly turned and said, "Nevertheless at your word I will cast out and let down the net" (Luke 5:5).

For Simon and his companions to catch fish, they had to drop their nets into the water, slowly make their way around the lake, and then draw up the nets to gather their catch. The awesome miracle Jesus was about to make manifest is the fact that they never toiled in the boat. The nets were dropped and then lifted back up. Luke 5:6 tells us that the quantity of fish was so large that the catch began to break the nets. What a great object lesson: obedience to Christ, even when it may seem farfetched, can produce a blessing with miracles, signs, and wonders.

You may need to stop and ask yourself, "What I am doing, or not doing, that is keeping me from my immediate blessing?" Just do a self-evaluation to see if you are walking in obedience or disobedience. What was the last thing the Lord ask you to do? Did you agree or disagree?

~~~~~ Ship 1 ~~~~~

In Luke 5:6–7 we read: "And when they had done this, they caught a great number of fish, and their net was breaking. So they signaled to their partners in the other boat to come and help them. And they came and filled both the boats, so that they began to sink."

The King James Version Bible does not refer to these vessels as boats, but instead, as ships. This will be the first of four ships that we will be discussing in this book. The ship was designed to hold fish as well as to transport people between two points. When Simon saw the number of fish in his net, he fell to his knees and began to repent.

First, he asked Jesus to leave his presence. This is a normal response of the in-the-flesh human. The flesh does not want to be around Jesus because He is a reminder of the sinful nature of man. In teaching the church how to reach beyond its doors, it must be understood that sin hates being exposed into the light. When Simon blurted out, "I am a sinful man," his fleshly nature was immediately exposed. The church's compassion for the lost must be the same as that of Jesus, which is one of love and not condemnation.

The one who brings condemnation is the devil, not the loving church of Jesus Christ! If I had been present, I would have explained to Simon, "Do not be afraid of what you have just seen.

This is about to become the new normal in your life. From now on, what you have witnessed with these fish, you are going to declare with men and women."

Jesus painted one of the most beautiful pictures of salvation on a large scale. You need to see this with eyes wide open. The ship is the representation of the church. He didn't just step into a fishing vessel. It was designed from the beginning that Jesus would use this vessel as a clear picture of the soon-to-come church. We need an awakening and revival on a personal level, as well as a corporate level back in the Church of America.

When Jesus steps into your ship—church—and you are obedient to His word, this fishing thing becomes easy. Jesus shows us right off the bat that it won't be a one-church awakening; rather, all the churches will have to come together in the laboring process of the great harvest. The unity of the church is a kingdom principle of the Lord.

In Ephesians 4:1–6, we read:

> I, therefore, the prisoner of the Lord, beseech you to walk worthy of the calling with which you were called, with all lowliness and gentleness, with longsuffering, bearing with one another in love, endeavoring to keep the unity of the Spirit in the bond of peace. There is one body and one Spirit, just as you were called in one hope of your calling; one Lord, one faith, one baptism; one God and Father of all, who is above all, and through all, and in you all.

You will see more of this scripture as we take this journey together. I want you to look closely at the word *endeavoring*.

In *Strong's Exhaustive Concordance of the Bible*, by James Strong, the word *endeavoring* is number 4706: "σπουδαιότερον spŏudaiŏtĕrŏn, spoo-dah-yot´-er-on; neut. of 4707 as adv.; more earnestly than others), i.e. very promptly: —very diligently."

As a part of the church, we are instructed to more earnestly and promptly, with diligence, keep God's house in unity by being led by the Holy Spirit, who is our sealer in the bond of peace. Therefore, Simon had to call for people from the church down the street to come help with the overwhelming catch of fish. Jesus then turned His attention to Simon. Jesus told Simon not to be afraid.

You see, Jesus is not about to set you on a journey without dealing with some deep-rooted issues. This first issue is going to be removing fear from your life. Fear is in direct disobedience of faith. So, we must deal with the fear of the past.

According to 1 Corinthians 3:16, we are the temple of God. So Christ has stepped into our church and has taken His rightful spot. According to 1 John 1:9, "If we confess our sins, He is faithful and just to forgive us our sins and to cleanse us from all unrighteousness."

This is the cleansing power of God over your past. Now, your present walk in Christ Jesus can be found in Colossians 2:6, which says, "As you therefore have received Christ Jesus the Lord, so walk in Him."

Our walk (life) is being led by the Holy Spirit the same way Jesus was led by the Holy Spirit. In 2 Timothy 1:7 we read, "For

God has not given us a spirit of fear, but one of power and of love and of a sound mind." This takes care of your past, present, and future endeavors; know that God is for you. Simon's attention was then turned away from looking at fish as just fish. Jesus used the fish, while standing in the church (the ship), as an analogy: those fish represented humans. The fish were not in the ship! The net was thrown outside the ship (the four walls of the church) in order to receive a catch. This catch was too big for one ship (church) to handle, so unity in the Holy Spirit had to be spread abroad so the church (all churches) could participate in the laboring and hauling in the harvest.

Watch this! After this incredible display of glory, a decision was made before the ships made dock. Jesus asked one simple question, "Follow me?" When the ships docked, Simon, James, and John, the sons of Zebedee, forsook all they had and followed Jesus. Their response was the same as the one my fellow paratroopers made in airborne school. Whenever we heard the words, "Follow me," the response was, "Lead the way." Jesus is asking you, "Will you follow Me?"

While you read this book, it is my prayer that, as the Holy Spirit begins to speak to you in such a soft voice of understanding, you will obediently push out into deep waters and allow yourself to encounter the unveiling miracles of God time and time again. Why wait one second longer? Jesus is calling you! If you have not had the type of encounter that I am speaking of, then stop now and pray this prayer!

Encounter Prayer

Lord Jesus, I know that I am a sinner. I am in desperate need of a Savior. I have tried to live this life on my own for years and I have come to myself and understand that I need You. Forgive me of my sins. Live in me. Guide me and direct me by your Holy Spirit. I surrender my life to you today.

Two

Pursuing The King

In the first chapter, I told the story about how I was in church and said a prayer that set me on my journey. In ministry, I see this a lot and understand the difference in saying a prayer and deciding to allow God to turn your life around. Davi and I were married and quickly found out we were pregnant with our daughter, Faith. Right after Faith was born, I began to be tormented by the enemy on a daily basis. Now, I can look back and see that the enemy was trying to destroy our family in its infancy the same way he slithered himself into the garden of Eden, destroyed the children of Moses' day, and had babies slaughtered in the search for the Christ.

Anger became my go-to for an outlet of frustration. In December of 2000, I found myself sitting in the Caddo County jail. That was my Jonah-in-the-whale moment. I was running from God while decaying on the inside. My recovery was a long process, but, man, was it worth it.

In 2001, I was employed at a metal fabrication company in Shreveport, Louisiana, as an overhead crane operator.

Unfortunately, this position was not cutting the mustard when it came to finances. I had just given my life to the Lord for real and was chasing after Him. During this process of looking for employment elsewhere, even asking personal friends for job-search help, I stumbled upon a great opportunity to go to work for Halliburton.

The qualification for the position of fluids engineer was a four-year degree in chemical engineering or five years of oilfield experience. I unfortunately had neither. But, God! The interview process was set up with a series of tests that had to be completed before an applicant could even qualify for an interview with a person. After taking the test, I was told that, if I was selected due to the test results, I would receive a follow-up phone call.

Walking out of the office, I kind of wrote myself off and thought, *There is no way I will be receiving that phone call, basically due to the fact that I knew absolutely nothing on the test.* The next day, to my surprise, the phone rang, and I was asked to go in for a follow-up interview. That interview led to me packing up and living in Houston, Texas, for the next three months where I attended their engineering school.

Dictionary.com defines the word *achievement* as "a thing done successfully, typically by effort, courage, or skill."

I didn't have any skills in this new field that I was embarking on. I did, however, have courage and a willingness to put in some effort. This was not an easy school by any means. I wanted this badly! I had to follow twenty other people through the process of the class, learning as I went along. Remember, most of these people already had degrees or had spent many years in the oil field. I followed my teacher closely and studied day and night, putting my nose to the grindstone. Three months later, I graduated engineering school and went from making roughly $600 a week to nearly six figures a year. There is something about the pursuit of God that changes things in the natural here on this earth.

In Mark 1:17–18, we read, "Then Jesus said to them, 'Follow Me, and I will make you become fishers of men.' They immediately left their nets and followed Him."

I want to elaborate on these two verses and advise you that, when Jesus says, "Follow me," it's not just an invitation, it's an opportunity for greatness. We live in a society today in which few people want to follow anybody. Everyone wants to be an instantaneous leader. The only issue with this is that, if you learn to become a great follower, then you will excel in becoming a successful leader. Successful leaders of today were first excellent followers. Success is also determined by whom you are following. Following a bad leader produces bad leadership in you. This is another one of those self-evaluations we must take by asking the hard questions. "Is this the tutelage that I want to subject myself to? Even though I know that I will pick up the characteristics and integrate them into my leadership." With that being said, we also have the flip side which doesn't have the fullness of walking in faith.

When the pastor of a church stands up to give direction to the congregation, parishioners may respond with questions: Where are we going? How long is it going to take? What's it going to cost me? Are we there yet?

All these questions should be weighed out with whomever is

a part of the guiding factors of the church, and then, with great confidence, answers should be unveiled before the congregation. The only problem is that those who ask these types of questions either have an authority issue or they have no faith!

"What are you getting at, Chris?" you may ask.

Jesus asked the disciples if they would pursue him. Will you make an effort to secure and attain what it is that I'm trying to teach you? Because I want you to reach your goal. I want you to achieve something greater than yourself. I want you to accomplish the things on earth that I am about to show you can be done, the things I will impart into your life. This is the only way that you will ever become an incredible leader. You inevitably must first become an excellent follower.

In *Strong's Exhaustive Concordance of the Bible*, the Greek word for "to follow" is 1205: "δεῦτε dĕutĕ, dyoo´-teh; from 1204 and an imper. form of εἶμι ĕimi (to go); come hither!:—come, × follow."

In James 4:8, we read, "Draw near to God and He will draw near to you. Cleanse your hands, you sinners; and purify your hearts, you double-minded."

Most people I encounter on a daily basis are overly concerned with what they may have to give up in order to follow Jesus. The reward of Christ is far greater than anything this world has to offer. That's why it's called faith. In 2 Corinthians 5:7, we learn: "For we walk by faith, not by sight."

Although, in this day and age, it's hard for people to walk by faith because they are so concerned with being able to see where they are going. In October 2016, at a Friday-night high school football game, I walked by a man I had known for a couple of years, named Mike. Prior to crossing paths with Mike that night, I had been pastor to students and families for 15 years, between two different churches. I sat down next to him started to share with him what was going on in my life.

He said these words to me, "So, you say that you're called to evangelism?"

I immediately replied, "Yes. I believe that God has called me into full-time evangelism."

To which Mike said, "Well, if this is true, then meet me at this address Monday morning at six o'clock."

Saturday and Sunday went by. On Monday morning I woke up early and made my way to Cleveland, Tennessee. I arrived at the designated church at six o'clock in the morning to meet with Mike. He sat me down in a little office area and began to speak to me. "When you sat down next to me at the football game, the Holy Spirit spoke to me and said, 'I will not waste your time with this one.'" So, Mike told me that, if I really wanted to be an evangelist, or even if I say that I had been called to be an evangelist, and I wanted to operate in the gifts, then I was to meet him there for the next week at six every morning.

I remember sitting there not saying a word. He flipped through the scriptures showing me verse upon verse, and then he said, "Let's go." Only I didn't hear, "Let's go"; rather, I heard the words, *"Follow Me."* And my response was what I had learned in my time in the military: "Lead the way." For the next three hours, we prayed. We prayed in the Holy Spirit (tongues) and prayed in the natural. (I thought I was going to die from praying for three hours straight!)

That one week taught me so much about how to pray, how to seek the Word of God, how to understand the case studies that have been given to me from Genesis to Revelation. I cherish those mornings. On the last day, Mike handed me a key and said, "Now, if you really want this, then you come on your own, and you'll do this for the next year." I decided to take a chance and pursue something that I wanted to attain.

Of course, the relationship between Mike and me is an amazing one. I greatly love and cherish every moment of it. What I really needed was to get closer to my Father in heaven. My pursuit was not after achievement; it was only after Him.

Now, with that being said, I am not a rogue evangelist who has no covering or church home. I attend Redemption to the Nations in Chattanooga, Tennessee, which is pastored by Kevin and Devin Wallace. I am ordained through the ministry of my spiritual Father who is also a spiritual covering in my life. Having these spiritual coverings gives me the liberties to pursue Christ and be sent into the nations. Let me give you a few scriptures to guide you on your pursuit.

> But seek first the kingdom of God and His righteousness, and all these things shall be added to you. (Matthew 6:33)

> Do you not know that those who run in a race all run, but one receives the prize? Run in such a way that you may obtain it. (1 Corinthians 9:24)

Therefore we also, since we are surrounded by so great a cloud of witnesses, let us lay aside every weight, and the sin which so easily ensnares us, and let us run with endurance the race that is set before us, looking unto Jesus, the author and finisher of our faith, who for the joy that was set before Him endured the cross, despising the shame, and has sat down at the right hand of the throne of God. (Hebrews 12:1–2)

The second book of Corinthians reminds us that "for we walk by faith, not by sight" (2 Corinthians 5:7). This pursuit, or the act of pursuing, after Jesus is a complete faith walk. As I am writing this, I remember the overtaking fear that gripped me the day my steady paycheck stopped. My thoughts were ambushed with doubt: *How am I going to provide for my family? How will I continue to send my daughter to a Christian school? Pay the bills?*

God is so good! I can say that this faith walk has taught me so much, including understanding Proverbs 3:5: "Trust in the Lord with all your Heart and lean not on your own understanding." Dictionary.com defines the word *pursuit* as "to follow close upon, catch or to come after in the act of pursuing to attain something or accomplish something." We know that the pursuit of Jesus is going to take faith. Hebrews 11:1: "Now faith is the substance of things hoped for, the evidence of things not seen."

Two words here that really stick out to me are *substance* and *evidence*. So, say you were driving downtown in your vehicle and were pulled over by the police. The police had probable cause to search your vehicle, and they found a controlled substance. That substance would then be the very evidence against you to convict you to some time in jail. Correct? So, if Christianity were on trial right now, and you were brought before a judge and jury, would enough substance of Christ be found in you—in other words, evidence—to "convict" you of being a Christian? Faith is a life of substance that produces hard evidence in favor for Jesus Christ. Can people see the Christ in you? This comes only by following closely. Romans 10:17: "So then faith comes by hearing, and hearing by the word of God."

I would like to ask you, how do you read your Bible? Do you read silently or out loud? When you read silently, you read faster and tend to skip vital information. When you read out loud, you read more slowly and hear yourself reading. Look at what the scripture says in Romans 10:8: "But what does it say? 'The word is near you, in your mouth and in your heart,'" (That is, the word of faith that we preach.)

Most people believe only half of what they see and a quarter of what they hear. Although they will believe 100 percent of what they say because they said it. They believe it because it came out of their mouths, even if what they said were lies! Romans 10:17 informs us, "Faith comes by hearing and hearing by the Word." Now, that does not mean when someone else is reading it to you on Sunday morning! When *you* read the Word, it comes out of your mouth, goes into your ears, and then is engrafted onto your heart. The Word, which is Jesus, is then closer to you than He has ever been. You have been quoting what God has breathed. This is why scripture says, in Proverbs 7:3, "Bind them on your fingers; Write them on the tablet of your heart."

~~~~~~ Ship 2 ~~~~~~

This brings me to our second ship encounter, the Ship (church) of Faith. Your faith is being tested on a daily basis. In Mark 4:35–41, we read:

On the same day, when evening had come, He said to them, "Let us cross over to the other side." Now when they had left the multitude, they took Him along in the boat as He was. And other little boats were also with Him. And a great windstorm arose, and the waves beat into the boat, so that it was already filling. But He was in the stern, asleep on a pillow. And they awoke Him and said to Him, "Teacher, do You not care that we are perishing?" Then He arose and rebuked the wind, and said to the sea, "Peace, be still!" And the wind ceased and there was a great calm. But He said to them, "Why are you so fearful? How is it that you have no faith?" And they feared exceedingly, and said to one another, "Who can this be, that even the wind and the sea obey Him!

When I hear the words in Mark 4:35, "let us cross over to the other side," I am accompanied with relief knowing that the words *let us* mean that Jesus is in the ship. For whatever reason, this statement did not give the disciples any confidence at all. The great storm arose, the waves beat at the side of the boat, and the boat began to fill with water. The disciples were scared, and Jesus was sound asleep. I find it quite funny that, while we think it is a total catastrophe, Jesus was chilled.

So, as they woke Jesus up, He stood on the bow of the boat and rebuked the storm with these words, "Peace be Still!" *Strong's Exhaustive Concordance of the Bible* tells us that the Greek word for "peace" here is *siopao*, which means to "silence, hush, properly, to be silent, hold one's peace." "To be still," in *Strong's Exhaustive Concordance of the Bible*, is the Greek word *phimoo*, which means "to close the mouth with a muzzle." I guess when Jesus wakes up, as any of us do from a sound sleep state, He literally says to the storm, "Shut up!"

Then, He turned His attention to the disciples and spoke to them with a very stern comment. He didn't say, "You have *little* faith." He said to the disciples, "You have *no* faith" (Mark 4:40). Fear contradicts faith. When you are walking in fear, it is as if you have no faith. May I remind you that Jesus is in your ship? He is living in you—at your home, at your work, at your school, on your street.

This life journey we are endeavoring to complete is not a lonesome walk through a dismal world. He is with you when you listen to His voice and are obedient to His words. If He says, "Let's go to the other side together," you need to strap on your life vest tightly and understand that you're going to make it to the other side. Hear me! You are going to make it! Pursue Him, be led by Him, and enjoy the ride of your life.

Three

Stay In The Boat

B oating was a pastime that I dearly loved. On the weekends, my family would venture out to Lake Tyler, in Tyler, Texas, to enjoy the benefits of nature. My dad had a Skeeter bass boat with a 115 Yamaha engine on it. Now, Dad was a fisherman and so was my Papaw. I was not a fisherman! I truly believe that, if attention-deficit/hyperactivity disorder (ADHD) had been recognized when I was growing up, then I would have been medicated to the gills. Unfortunately, behavior that is now attributed to ADHD was considered just "bad" back then, and many kids received "medication" in the form of leather belts. I would take two daily and have no one to call in the morning.

One particular day was, as I remember, a hot Texas Saturday. My dad drove the boat out to his honey hole of a fishing spot. Then he dropped the trolling motor into the water so he could sneak up on the massive fish we were about to catch. As he looked for fish intently in his depth finder, he told us to get the pole ready to start fishing.

Fishing is kind of like hunting deer, which I love to do.

Although, I think fishing should be called "sitting around waiting patiently to catch a fish." Just like it should be called "sitting and waiting for deer" instead of hunting deer. Hunting means that you are pursuing your prey. Sitting in a tree in thirty-degree temperatures waiting for the deer to show up is called "waiting." I was an off-the-wall-kid who hated sitting and waiting, so fishing was not my strong suit.

I didn't want to *fish*. I wanted to *catch*! And if we were not catching fish, I was board in about five seconds. I began to whine. "Dad, its hot! Let's get in the water! Dad, let's go skiing!" Then, he said it: "Okay, boy!" Dad threw the poles into the boat, hooked up the ski eye pole, and said, "Have at it, boy!" What happened next was not my dad's fault, but he did take credit for it.

I learned to water ski on flat wooden skis, which was what I was using that day. My dad proceeded to speed up the boat, and I loved going fast! My left ski began to do something out of the ordinary—it began to violently shake left and right. Suddenly, the ski split right down the center. As this was taking place, I was trying to ski on my right ski, but to no avail. That ski somehow decided to come out of the water at a high rate of speed and hit me in my nether region.

Water in my ears! Water in my nose! Water in my mouth! I was sure I had drunk half the lake that day. What had happened? The rudder on my left ski had broken off, splintering the ski in half. The other ski had just hurt me badly, or so I thought. When my dad pulled over to me, he looked at me. Of course, I thought I was drowning. He said, "Uh huh! Next time you'll stay in the boat, won't ya?" I simply replied, "Yes, sir."

~~~~~~ Ship 3 ~~~~~~

Whether we are following, leading, or sending it all comes back to obedience. I love the story in Matthew 14:22. Jesus sent His disciples across the Sea of Galilee as He ascended a mountain for prayer:

> Immediately Jesus made His disciples get into the boat and go before Him to the other side, while He sent the multitudes away. And when He had sent the multitudes away, He went up on the mountain by Himself to pray. Now when evening came, He was alone there. But the boat was now in the middle of the sea, tossed by the waves, for the wind was contrary. Now in the fourth watch of the night Jesus went to them, walking on the sea. And when the disciples saw Him walking on the sea, they were troubled, saying, "It is a ghost!" And they cried out for fear. But immediately Jesus spoke to them, saying, "Be of good cheer! It is I; do not be afraid." And Peter answered Him and said, "Lord, if it is You, command me to come to You on the water." So He said, "Come." And when Peter had come down out of the boat, he walked on the water to go to Jesus. But when he saw that the wind was boisterous, he was afraid; and beginning to sink he cried out, saying, "Lord, save me!" And immediately Jesus stretched out His hand and caught him, and

said to him, "O you of little faith, why did you doubt?" And when they got into the boat, the wind ceased.

This is where this story is about to get very interesting. Now I want you to come at it as if this is the first time you have ever heard it. Mark tells us that, as the disciples were journeying across the sea, Jesus saw them straining and rowing due to the storm that was around them. This should give you and me great hope that, no matter where we are, Jesus has His vision on us, and He knows exactly what we are going through.

No matter what your storm may be in this very moment in time, Jesus knows right where you are, and He has his sights on you. As evening fell, Jesus went up on the mountain to pray. Verses 23–24 tell us that Jesus saw that the disciples were in the middle of the storm. It would have been around seven o'clock in the evening when Jesus went to pray and saw the disciples struggling. The scripture goes on to say, in verse 25, that the fourth watch of the night was when Jesus descended down the mountain and begam to walk on the water.

The fourth watch is between three and six in the morning. So, get this—I need you to understand something. Jesus saw them struggling at seven o'clock the night before but waited eight hours before He made His journey to the other side. Mark also tells us that, as Jesus walked on the water, He would have passed them by. Mark 6:48: "Then He saw them straining at rowing, for the wind was against them. Now about the fourth watch of the night He came to them, walking on the sea, and would have passed them by."

The disciples saw something in the distance. I am not sure exactly how far Jesus was from the disciples. According to Quora. com, on a boat you can, with the naked eye, see another boat crest the horizon at twelve miles. Jesus is not as big as a ship, but this should give you some insight: you can see a long distance on the water. The scripture lets us know that He was so far away, they perceived Him to be a ghost.

The disciples had to yell in order to hear each other. When they made verbal contact, Peter decided to speak up and shout out to Jesus, "If it is You." Peter's remark is another clue that Jesus was far off. Try and wrap your mind around the fact that Peter was relying upon what he heard instead of what he could see. This is why in scripture thirteen times we see, "He who has an ear to hear let him hear." I can't strictly rely upon what I see. I must fine tune my ear to hear the Holy Spirit speak, so when He does, I know His voice without a shadow of a doubt.

In Matthew 14: 28–29, Peter calls out to Jesus, "Lord, if it is You, command me to come to You on the water." So, He says, "Come." Peter's response came in two parts. First, he asked if the person they can see was Jesus. Then he made a request: he asked, if the answer to his question is yes, would Jesus command him to come on the water with Him. Jesus was not about to deny Himself! His response to Peter, to paraphrase, was, "It's me, Jesus, and if you want to come out here, then come on."

Here is where we are going to shake some things up that you have heard in the past. Watch this! The Bible says that, while Peter was in the boat, the winds were contrary. The Greek word for "contrary," according to *Strong's Exhaustive Concordance of the*

Bible, is *enantios*, and it is defined as "winds beating against the boat." Peter chose to leave the safety of the ship that Jesus put him into to make it to the next destination. "If you want to come out here so bad, then come on!"

Everyone preaches this as you have to have faith to get out of the boat and walk on the water with Jesus. If walking on water was so great, then why was Peter about to start sinking? Here's a theory! Maybe he was never supposed to get out of the boat in the first place. If Jesus was going to walk past them, then maybe He knew that they would make it to the other side. After all, Jesus said to get in the boat and go to the other side, didn't He?

I told you in Chapter 1 that the boat or ship was a representation of the church. When you step out of the safety and covering that the Lord has provided for you, the possibilities of sinking are inevitable. When Peter stepped out of the boat, the winds shifted, and so did the storm. While they were in the boat, the winds were contrary. When Peter stepped out of the boat, the winds become boisterous.

Matthew 14:29–30: "So He said, 'Come.' And when Peter had come out of the boat, he walked on the water to go to Jesus. But when he saw that the wind was boisterous, he was afraid; and beginning to sink he cried out, saying, 'Lord, save me.'"

The gentle wind that rocked the boat turned into a boisterous wind. *Strong's Exhaustive Concordance of the Bible* tells us that the Greek word for "boisterous" is *ischyros*, which means the "wind become strong, mighty and violent." So the wind might be bad while you're in the church, but if you step out of the safety of your church covering, hurricane-force winds hit in every direction.

Peter stepped out of the boat. The winds became boisterous. He then became afraid and began to sink.

I want you to slow down and focus on what I'm saying. This means that, in the moment when Peter was sinking, Jesus did nothing. According to dictionary.com, the word *beginning* means "the point in time or space when something begins." There is a time lapse here. Peter was sinking, and Jesus was still far off. It's not until Peter cried out and said, "Lord, save me," that Jesus was close to him. Immediately, Jesus was in the presence of Peter. He reached down and pulled him up out of the boisterous storm and set him back in the boat where he belonged. No matter how far you may feel from Jesus, with one cry you will be in his presence, immediately.

Here is why I don't believe Peter was supposed to exit the boat. Verse 22 reveals a couple of interesting points. First, Jesus made His disciples get into the boat and go before Him to the other side. The New King James Version says that Jesus *made* them. The King James Version says that Jesus *constrained* them. This Greek word for "constrain," found in *Strong's Exhaustive Concordance of the Bible*, is *anagkazō*, which means "to necessitate, compel, drive to, constrain by force, threats, by permission, entreaties, our by other means." This lets me know that the disciples did not want to leave Jesus's side. Jesus had to force them to enter the boat, and He declared that He would meet them on the other side.

Second, Jesus told them to go before Him to the other side. This is the sending, or marching, order the Lord has given to us to go: "Go, and I am with you even if you think you're by yourself." If the Lord has sent you, then He is going to make sure you reach your destination unharmed. He will also be there with you because that is what He said He would do. You might be going through a storm right now. The last thing you want to do is exit the position the Lord has given you. Only in proper position can you be sure you will reach your destiny.

The scripture says that, when Peter reentered the boat, the wind stopped. What actually happened was that Jesus placed him back where he belonged. It doesn't matter how far away Jesus may seem or feel to you. He can show up immediately and pull you out of whatever you are sinking into. Next, if you find yourself outside the fellowship and the covering of the church, then He will put you back where you are supposed to be in the safety of the body.

Have you identified your location while reading this chapter? Have you found yourself outside the safety of the covering of Jesus? Here is the awesome thing about Jesus: He didn't make the disciples go back and start their journey over. When He placed Peter safe and sound back in the boat, they continued with the ministry at hand.

You might need to let Jesus put you back where you belong— back in fellowship with Jesus, back in fellowship with His church and His people. This is what I love about Jesus. He picked up His disciples, put them back on the right path, and they continued with the mission. Isn't it time for you to be back in your position so you can continue with the mission that Christ has given you?

Peter and the other disciples had no clue as to what was about to happen, or what they were about to see. Over the next three years, Peter was privileged to be a part of miracle after miracle: healing a paralytic, raising a ruler's daughter from the dead, healing a hemorrhaging woman, feeding the five thousand, feeding the four thousand, cursing a fig tree, raising an epileptic boy, raising a widow's son, healing a nobleman's son of a fever, raising Lazarus from the dead, healing the blind eyes and deaf ears.

What about the teachings and the parables that they learned: new wine in old wineskins, sowing and reaping, mustard seed faith, the hidden treasures, the pearl of great price, the lost sheep, the unforgiving servant, the workers in the vineyard, the rich fool, the barren fig tree, the great supper, the lost coin, the lost son, the rich man and Lazarus.

In this life of following and pursuing, it is faith that is leading us. Today is the day you get closer to Jesus as you continue in your effort to attain what He has in store for you. When He asks, "Follow Me," will your response be, "Lead the way!"?

Four

The Process Of Transformation

A ccording to dictionary.com, the word *transformation* means "to change in form, appearance, nature, or character." I remember when the Lord spoke to me and said, "I'm going to remind you of my goodness on a daily basis by showing you yellow butterflies." Yellow is one of the most reflective colors in nature. To this day, I do all my note taking on yellow pads, which makes the black ink easier to see.

In Psalm 68:13, the Word says, "Though you lie down among the sheepfolds, You will be like the wings of a dove covered with silver, And her feathers with yellow gold."

Yellow here is in the representation of gold or something of great value. Yellow can also mean leprosy, but that is not the direction we are going. According to Biblestudy.org, the Bible tells us that the New Jerusalem created by God will have twelve foundations, and each one will shine a different kind of light based on a particular precious stone (Revelation 21:19) (www.biblestudy.

org/bible-study-by-topic/gemstones-in-the-bible/gems-in-new-jerusalem.html). The seventh foundation (seven is the number of perfection) has chrysolite within it—a yellowish-green or brown gemstone. *Strong's Exhaustive Concordance of the Bible* tells us that the Greek word translated as "chrysolite" means a gem that looks like the color gold or yellow.

This brings us to the butterfly. The butterfly does not start out as such. Shocker, I know! Unfortunately for the beautiful butterfly, it begins its life as a nasty, creepy, crawling, caterpillar. You may like them, and that's fine, but I find them hideous. The caterpillar must go through five processes of what is called molting before it is transformed into the beautiful butterfly.

The one process that I found very interesting was the chrysalis phase. In this phase, the caterpillar literally transforms into a liquid goo before it becomes a butterfly. This entire process is called metamorphosis. Dictionary.com defines the word *metamorphosis* as "a profound change in form from one stage to the next in the life history of an organism, as from the caterpillar to the pupa and from the pupa to the adult butterfly." It is also defined as "any complete change in appearance, character, circumstances, etc." (No extra charge for the science lesson!)

During the chrysalis phase, the pupa is at its most vulnerable stage. The caterpillar must give itself over to this process of transformation. During this stage, if you were to open the cocoon, you would find nothing more than a gooey mess. This just so happens to be an excellent picture of what a sinner goes through in the process of becoming a Christian.

We start out as ugly, creepy, crawling, sinners. We become

completely undone by the power of God. In this process, we must be completely vulnerable about surrendering our past junk to the Lord. This is what causes the pupil to become mush before the Lord as He begins the next process of restoration. In Romans 12:1–2, we read:

> I beseech you therefore, brethren, by the mercies of
> God, that you present your bodies a living sacrifice,
> holy, acceptable to God, which is your reasonable
> service. And do not be conformed to this world, but
> be transformed by the renewing of your mind, that
> you may prove what is that good and acceptable and
> perfect will of God.

On that summer day, I was one of the assistant football coaches for my daughter Faith's varsity high school team. That afternoon, before the players came out of the field house, I was sitting in a dugout (our field was a multi-purpose field). I was by myself, and the Lord surprised me with hundreds of yellow butterflies. They flew over the football field in a majestic manner that took my breath away.

One butterfly alighted on the top of the field house and remained there during the entire practice. I was mesmerized to say the least. That was the day that I knew the Lord was calling me to full-time evangelism. All summer long, every day, I would see yellow butterflies somewhere around me. How awesome is it that our Father in heaven would use something as small and downright vulnerable to prove His point?

An article on the Butterfly Fun Facts website tells us that most caterpillars don't even make it to become butterflies! (butterfly-fun-facts.com/only-1-or-2-butterfly-eggs-out-of-100-live-to-become-adult-butterflies) They are eaten by other insects or die because of harsh environments. Isn't it crazy that God would use something so fragile to be a message of hope and transformation into who you and I were always meant to be? Beautiful and flying in the heavens.

Be transformed!

In Matthew 16:13–19, Jesus turned to his disciples:

> When Jesus came into the region of Caesarea Philippi, he asked his disciples, saying, "Who do men say that I, the Son of Man, am?" So they said, "Some say John the Baptist, some Elijah, others Jeremiah one of the prophets." He said to them, "But who do you say that I am?" Simon Peter answered and said, "You are the Christ, the son of the living God." Jesus answered and said to him," Blessed are you, Simon bar Jonah, for flesh and blood is not revealed this to you, but my father who is in heaven. And I also say to you that you are Peter, and on this rock I will build my church, and the gates of Hades shall not prevail against it. And I will give you the keys of the kingdom of heaven, and whatever you bind on earth will be bound in heaven, and whatever you loose on earth will be loosed in heaven."

There was a transformation that took place here that changed a man's nature and character. Dictionary.com gives one definition for metamorphosis as "any complete change in appearance, character, circumstances." To be transformed or go through a transformation means to change in form, appearance, nature, or character. This is a perfect picture of the old man passing away and all things becoming new.

In 2 Corinthians 5:17 we read: "Therefore, if anyone is in Christ, he is a new creation; old things have passed away; behold, all things have become new."

Jesus asked the question, "Who am I?" His disciples began to answer what other people have said, "Well, some say you are that, and some say that you are this." (Side note: This is an epidemic in the church; it is regurgitating what we have heard instead of declaring what we have sought after ourselves.) Don't get me wrong, there are many great men and women of God in this world who have spoken incredible words—words that have changed my life. And at times, I may even quote them.

The struggle today is that there are more people quoting people than quoting the Word of God. Repeating things that you have heard, without researching the source, is a very scary endeavor. When you do this, you don't even know if what was communicated to you was even truthful. I always make a point somewhere in my preaching to emphasize researching and seeking the Word rather than just taking others'—including my own—word for it.

My responsibility is to encourage and equip the saints as well as to place a hunger deep down inside of you for the Word of God. This will produce a desire in you to become more of a student of the Word. Chase after the Word studies! Let them lead you deep into the mysteries that the Lord wants to unveil to you.

Why do I believe what I believe?

Back to the disciples. "I call you this name because I have heard others call you this." This is all I know to call you because I don't have a relationship with you. If I was in true relationship with you, then I would know who you are.

I would know all your names! I would know that you are Advocate, Lamb of God, The Resurrection and the Life, Alpha and Omega, King of Kings, Lord of Lords, Wonderful Counselor, Prince of Peace, the Great I Am, Immanuel, Messiah, the Word, Savior, Author and Finisher of our Faith, Redeemer, Lion of the Tribe of Judah, the Way, the Truth, the Life, Jesus Christ!

Then in verse15, Jesus gets personal and says, "But who do you say that I am?" Simon speaks up and says, "You are the Christ, the son of the living God." Jesus then turns to Simon and begins to bless him. With this blessing comes the metamorphosis and transformation of Simon. To paraphrase: "Peter you are blessed! You are going to preach the gospel. You are going see lives changed and transformed in the very manner that you are being rebirthed right now, due to your faith in Me. These things are not going to happen just because you possess the correct answer to my question. It will be because my Father in heaven has revealed to you who I am. Your attention to having an ear to hear will be one quality that is needed to understand direction in this Kingdom walk. Now, I'm going to reveal to you who you are. You are no longer Simon the fishermen. You are no longer a man with no hope. You are no longer a wretched individual. You are no longer the old man that I met on that boat. You are Peter the Rock. You are *petros*, a rock or stone. Peter you're going to be a part of helping build My church, and the gates of hell are not going to prevail against it. So, I'm giving to you the keys of the Kingdom of Heaven." Understand that what I'm saying right now is also for you! Those who are believers in Christ Jesus. You are a part of building this church. For if you are a child of God, then you are the church."

God is giving you the keys of the Kingdom of Heaven so that whatever you bind on earth is bound in heaven, and whatever you loose on earth is loosed in heaven. You see, when you receive Christ as your Lord and Savior, your life begins to change. Or should I say transforms. The people that I used to run with would make statements like, "You don't look the same anymore." "You don't communicate the same anymore or even like doing the same things anymore." "A transformation has taken place in your life."

What does building the church even look like? In you, as the Temple of God, it is forever growing in greater intimacy with the Father. Knowing His word is knowing Him. Private devotion time with just you and Jesus builds layer upon layer of increased faith. This is where you will see your faith go from glory to glory, from faith to faith.

Certain things that you used to do no longer take precedence in your life. Spending time with the Father has become the most important factor in my life. Where we used to chase after worldly desires, now we find ourselves chasing after Kingdom concepts. The Kingdom atmosphere we seek after is the very pursuit of God's Heart. We serve such a good Father that He is faithful and just, and His perfect will is to bless His children. You're no longer the old man; you are a new creation in Christ Jesus!

Transformation comes with great responsibility.

With this transformation comes a great responsibility because we are given possession of the keys to the Kingdom. Firstly, Kingdom keys can't stay in your pocket. Secondly, Kingdom keys were never meant to be paraded around on your belt loop so everyone knows you are in charge. Kingdom keys are meant to accomplish two things: lock and unlock—to lock the doors that no person should enter and unlock the doors that all people can enter into.

Every day we are approached with opportunities to lock or unlock doors, to bind up or loose. I see the Holy Spirit as the sheriff of the trinity. We have Kingdom keys to arrest the lost and set the captives free from their bondage and chains.

At a church service in Arkansas, I began to prophesy over a woman who had three prodigal children. I spoke to her and let her know that she had the Holy Ghost Sheriff on her side. If she wanted her children to come home, then she only needed to call the sheriff to arrest them and bring them home. The Lord said to me, "Speak to her and let her know that, before she leaves the church today, all three of her kids will come home." I did as I heard the Lord say.

That evening, she came back to the night service wanting desperately to give a testimony. She began to explain about the prophetic word and how she had been outside standing on the top step of the church. Suddenly, her phone rang. It was her first child asking for permission to come home. When she finished that conversation, and hung up the phone, her second child called and said, "I'm coming home." By the time she reached the bottom step, all three of her children had called. They came home that day and had dinner with their mother. Call out what you need and ask the Sheriff Holy Ghost to arrest what you need and bring it home!

Has there been a transformation in your life? This transformation experience is about to unlock the true identity of the person Christ has always intended for you to be. The Lord gave me my life scripture during my transformation. It is what I refer to when I don't feel capable of walking in the calling for which I was called.

In 2 Timothy 4:1–5 we read:

> I charge you therefore before God and the Lord Jesus Christ, who will judge the living and the dead at His appearing and His kingdom: Preach the word! Be ready in season and out of season. Convince, rebuke, exhort, with all longsuffering and teaching. For the time will come when they will not endure sound doctrine, but according to their own desires, because they have itching ears, they will heap up for themselves teachers; and they will turn their ears away from the truth and be turned aside to fables. But you be watchful in all things, endure afflictions, do the work of an evangelist, fulfill your ministry.

Fulfill your ministry!

The five scriptures I present in this chapter are a reminder to me of who God says I am! Not man, and definitely not Satan!

There was a great transformation that took place in my life. What about your transformation? What has God done in your life? Where has He brought you from? What has He called you to do? Are you doing it? Right now, acknowledge who Christ is. Let the metamorphosis process happen in you so you can be transformed into the beauty your God has always intended you to be. You have some keys in your pocket. Let's go unlock some heavenly doors!

Five

Destruction By Pride

G rowing up in east Texas, I was taught that you didn't take handouts. You work hard for your money by the sweat of your brow—no sweat, no moola. I was raised on a farm where we had cows, horses, chickens, and a garden. I didn't mind working with the animals.

Funny story—one morning my mother asked my sister to go and fetch (which means "gather" in Texan) some eggs for breakfast. The only problem with gathering eggs is that chickens are often nesting on the eggs. They don't want to get up! You must shoo the hens off the eggs or grab them by the tail feathers and pick them up off the eggs.

My sister, Wendi, went out to the door of the chicken coop and began to yell at the top of her lungs at the chickens. "You get up, chickens! Get off those eggs now, you dumb chickens!" One jumped off the roost and began to chase Wendi around the pen. Good times, good times.

Anyway, I would work the farm, mow the pasture, and tend the garden, which I especially hated. When I say hate, I mean I loathed it entirely. Nothing like wasting a whole Saturday breaking your back over a row of purple hull peas. Once the picking was done, we would go to the house, sit on the back porch, and shell them all day long. All we were left with was purple thumbs and a sore back—even though all adults know that kids don't receive a back until they are thirty years of age. A least that's what I was told.

This kind of work was long and hard. Not to mention, I think the wages were pretty off, if I say so myself. Wish I had known about child labor laws back then. I would mow the pasture for my granny for one dollar an acre in 1989. That came up to $100.

After I came home from the army in 1999, my granny asked me if I would mow the pasture for her. Of course, I would. Actually, I enjoyed mowing the pasture, getting outside in the sun and listening to my Walkman. (I just gave up my age with that statement.) After a couple of days, I finished mowing the hundred acres of pasture. I went to my granny's house, and she said, "Here you go." She handed me $100. Wait a minute! It was a $100 in 1989. Now it was 1999, and I still got $100. What's up with that? What about inflation! This was highway robbery! Ten years later, I should be looking at least $1000 or so. I knew the price of mowing the pasture was going to be $100. It had always been $100, and I knew deep down that it wasn't about to change. I really wanted more even though I knew that Granny had hired me to mow the pasture for $100.

In Matthew 20: 1–16, we read:

> For the kingdom of heaven is like a landowner who
> went out early in the morning to hire laborers for

his vineyard. Now when he had agreed with the laborers for a denarius a day, he sent them into his vineyard. And he went out about the third hour and saw others standing idle in the marketplace, and said to them, "You also go into the vineyard, and whatever is right I will give you." So, they went. Again he went out about the sixth and the ninth hour and did likewise. And about the eleventh hour he went out and found others standing idle, and said to them, "Why have you been standing here idle all day?" They said to him, "Because no one hired us." He said to them, "You also go into the vineyard, and whatever is right you will receive." So when evening had come, the owner of the vineyard said to his steward, "Call the laborers and give them their wages, beginning with the last to the first." And when those came who were hired about the eleventh hour, they each received a denarius. But when the first came, they supposed that they would receive more; and they likewise received each a denarius. And when they had received it, they complained against the landowner, saying, "These last men have worked only one hour, and you made them equal to us who have borne the burden and the heat of the day." But he answered one of them and said, "Friend, I am doing you no wrong. Did you not agree with me for a denarius? Take what is yours and go your way. I wish to give to this last man the same as to you. Is it not lawful for me to do what I wish with my own things? Or is your eye evil because I am good?" So the last will be first, and the first last. For many are called, but few chosen.

I can see myself in this hired hand. Wait a minute—I slaved all day long! I'm out there busting my butt for $100, and this dude gets to come out here and work one measly hour and he gets $100? If this happened today, then not only would there be rioting, but some people would take advantage and try to beat the system. "Dude, shut up! Just come out to work at the eleventh hour every day and get *paid*!"

That should let you know just how sick and twisted our humanistic minds can be.

This is what pride does. It's a creeper that is never satisfied and always looking for easy street. It never seems to surprise me that when people get promoted in a field, are asked to do a job, or receive some kind of accolades, it always tends to go straight to their heads. I'm talking hot air balloon–kind of stuff.

In Proverbs 16:18, we read, "Pride goes before destruction, And a haughty spirit before a fall."

In *Strong's Exhaustive Concordance of the Bible*, the Hebrew definition for pride is "exaltation, majesty, excellence of nations of God of the Jordan pride, arrogance, in the bad sense." Not all pride is bad. In this case, pride or arrogance comes before shattering and crushing ruin. Not long after the transformation that took place in Peter's life, we see another form working inside of him.

In Matthew 16:21, Jesus begins to predict His death and

resurrection. He explains how He will be killed and raised up on the third day. Then, in verse 22, Peter, who just got promoted to the position of the Rock, tries to intervene. Matthew 16:22–23: "Then Peter took Him aside and began to rebuke Him, saying, 'Far be it from You, Lord; this shall not happen to You!' But He turned and said to Peter, 'Get behind Me, Satan! You are an offense to Me, for you are not mindful of the things of God, but the things of men.'"

I can understand the zeal and passion of Peter in this moment. I would not put it past myself to probably have done the same thing. I can imagine Peter thinking, *I have spent all this time with You, and it has been the greatest experience of my life, not to mention the impartation that You just gave me. So let's fight this accusation.* Jesus was not as excited. When Jesus rebuked Peter, He was also rebuking Satan.

This is what we call the Law of Double Reference. In this scripture, Jesus is speaking directly to Peter while also speaking to Satan, who is using Peter to try to stop Jesus from going to the cross. Peter didn't know that he had become a pawn in this meeting with Jesus. So, what we have here is Peter in the natural sense, the flesh, and in the spiritual sense, being rebuked by Jesus. All the while, Jesus was addressing Satan in the spiritual sense for using Peter against Him.

Let me take this time to address the elephant in the room, which is whether Peter was possessed by the devil or not. Was Peter possessed by Satan in this scripture? The answer is no, he was not! Can a believer in Christ Jesus be possessed by Satan? The answer is no! Listen to what Jesus says to the Pharisee when asked about demons.

Now when the Pharisees heard it they said, "This fellow does not cast out demons except by Beelzebub, the ruler of the demons." But Jesus knew their thoughts and said to them: "Every kingdom divided against itself is brought to desolation, and every city or house divided against itself will not stand. If Satan casts out Satan, he is divided against himself. How then will his kingdom stand? And if I cast out demons by Beelzebub, by whom do your sons cast them out? Therefore, they shall be your judges. But if I cast out demons by the Spirit of God, surely the kingdom of God has come upon you. Or how can one enter a strong man's house and plunder his goods, unless he first binds the strong man? And then he will plunder his house. He who is not with Me is against Me, and he who does not gather with Me scatters abroad. (Matthew 12:24–30)

Jesus explains here that a house divided cannot stand. However, can Christians be oppressed or persuaded? Yes. Oppression is the feeling of being heavily burdened, mentally or physically, by troubles, adverse conditions, anxiety, and other negative conditions. Satan loves to use these attributes against the children of God to make them feel less than they should as children of God. I am sad to say that most Christians live their whole lives with mental burdens that paralyze them from living in fullness.

In James 1:6–8 we read, "But let him ask in faith, with no doubting, for he who doubts is like a wave of the sea driven and tossed by the wind. For let not that man suppose that he will receive anything from the Lord; he is a double-minded man, unstable in all his ways."

According *Strong's Exhaustive Concordance of the Bible*, this term *double-minded*, when translated from the Greek, means "to be divided in interest." This is how Satan uses division to bring separation between you and Jesus. It is the same way Satan tried to use division between Jesus and Peter. Another example was when Peter spoke with Cornelius about Jesus.

In Acts 10:38, we read: "How God anointed Jesus of Nazareth with the Holy Spirit and with power, who went about doing good and healing all who were oppressed by the devil, for God was with Him."

Dictionary.com defines the word *persuasion* as "to prevail on (a person) to do something, as by advising or urging: to induce to believe by appealing to reason or understanding; convince." This is the leading of the enemy instead of the leading of the Holy Spirit. Peter was under the persuasion of Satan to make the statement that he made. How is this possible while walking with Jesus? Satan will use reasoning in man's wisdom to invoke you to question the plans of Jesus.

We read in Acts 5:1–11:

> But a certain man named Ananias, with Sapphira
> his wife, sold a possession. And he kept back part
> of the proceeds, his wife also being aware of it, and
> brought a certain part and laid it at the apostles'
> feet. But Peter said, "Ananias, why has Satan filled

your heart to lie to the Holy Spirit and keep back part of the price of the land for yourself? While it remained, was it not your own? And after it was sold, was it not in your own control? Why have you conceived this thing in your heart? You have not lied to men but to God." Then Ananias, hearing these words, fell down and breathed his last. So great fear came upon all those who heard these things. And the young men arose and wrapped him up, carried him out, and buried him. Now it was about three hours later when his wife came in, not knowing what had happened. And Peter answered her, "Tell me whether you sold the land for so much?" She said, "Yes, for so much." Then Peter said to her, "How is it that you have agreed together to test the Spirit of the Lord? Look, the feet of those who have buried your husband are at the door, and they will carry you out." Then immediately she fell down at his feet and breathed her last. And the young men came in and found her dead, and carrying her out, buried her by her husband. So great fear came upon all the church and upon all who heard these things.

This was Satan using persuasion over people to bring ruin upon them or the works of Christ.

In 1 Corinthians 2:5 we read, "that your faith should not be in the wisdom of men but in the power of God."

A man once told me that I was so heavenly minded I was no

earthly good. What an asinine statement for someone to make. Jesus told us to pray for His Kingdom to come. Well, if the Kingdom is going to come, then someone is going to have to be Heavenly minded in order for the earth to receive these Kingdom-related works.

Have you ever found yourself weighing out scenarios in your head instead of taking them to prayer? Pride can creep its ugly self into our lives when we become more focused on our own agendas than on what God knows is the best plan. Peter received the rebuke, and Satan left. I can be the first to say that a rebuke by Jesus, or spiritual authority, can sometimes feel like death itself. In the grand scheme of things, I would much rather receive the rebuke, receive freedom, and see the devil hightail it out of my presence and my mind.

So how do we combat this spirit of pride? Humility! The essence of living in humility is the direct opposite of living in pride or arrogance. In 1 Peter 5:5 we learn that "God resists the proud, But gives grace to the humble."

Humility combats the error of pride. If God resists those who are prideful, then he must embrace those who are humble. Humility goes a long way when it comes to living as a Christian. In the Word, we are told that taking on humility is a virtue for the new human.

In Colossians 3:12–17, we learn:

> Therefore, as the elect of God, holy and beloved, put on tender mercies, kindness, humility, meekness, longsuffering; bearing with one another, and

forgiving one another, if anyone has a complaint against another; even as Christ forgave you, so you also must do. But above all these things put on love, which is the bond of perfection. And let the peace of God rule in your hearts, to which also you were called in one body; and be thankful. Let the word of Christ dwell in you richly in all wisdom, teaching and admonishing one another in psalms and hymns and spiritual songs, singing with grace in your hearts to the Lord. And whatever you do in word or deed, do all in the name of the Lord Jesus, giving thanks to God the Father through Him.

The scripture tells us to put on these attributes. In *Strong's Exhaustive Concordance of the Bible*, the Greek word for "put on" is *endyō*, which literally means "to sink into a garment, to invest with clothing (literally or figuratively):—array, clothe (with), endue, have (put) on." Paul is telling us that, if we are to live humbly before the Lord, and not in a prideful manner, then we have to cover ourselves with tender mercies. Clothe yourself with kindness, sink into humility, which embraces the fact that there should be less of us and more of Him. Slide into meekness and longsuffering, which is patience. Humility will kill every ounce of pride in your life. Don't let pride keep you from your mountaintop experience.

Six

Mountain Top

L et me just say that I love the mountains. Love! It is my
continual daily prayer to live on a peaceful and quiet mountain
somewhere. This is a daily prayer for deliverance from subdivision
mayhem! I desire to sit on the porch of a cabin, drinking my coffee,
reading my Bible, spending some time with Jesus, while looking
at the same view that the Lord sees. (Not to mention enough land
for hunting!)

One year, Davi and I had the privilege of taking a trip with
some close friends of ours, Clyde and Ann, to Winter Park,
Colorado. What a gorgeous, snow filled, wonderland that place
was. Our church at the time, in Shreveport, Louisiana, used this as
a family spring break getaway and a time of refreshing. We would
all ski during the day and have devotions, food, fellowship, coffee,
hot chocolate, and games at night.

One day we skied a track that led around the back side of
the mountain. This journey took us two hours out of the way of
civilization. I can't remember if it was a blue or black slope that
we were trying to traverse. All I remember was that it took a long

time to get back to where the smart people were enjoying their day of skiing.

Once we made it back to civilization, several of the guys wanted to take another shortcut through some moguls to head back to the cabins. I, on the other hand, decided to take the easy trail back to give my aching body some rest. As I journeyed through the tall trees covered in fresh powder from the recent snowfall, listening to the sounds of nature, something happened that I have never forgotten. I can remember this as if it happened yesterday.

The Easy Path

The mountain was to my right, and when I say to my right, I mean I could easily touch it with my hand without fully extending my arm. To my left was a roughly sixty-foot drop off the side of the mountain to a creek bed full of rocks and freezing water. The path itself was approximately five feet wide. This path was designated a green leisure trip. On this leisurely ski down to the bottom, I hit a patch of ice. Suddenly my skis turned left, and before I could react in any way, I went off the side of the mountain.

Six feet or more down, I found myself hanging onto a small oak tree no more than eight to ten inches in diameter. The thought went through my head, *What just happened? Did I just ski off the side of the mountain?* Before anyone asks the question, I did not own a cell phone at that time and would probably not have had service where I was dangling if I'd had one. Ten minutes passed, twenty minutes passed, forty minutes passed, and no one skied by on the leisure trail that I had decided to take.

I tried to pull myself up, but to no avail. I could not reach the top. I was praying the entire time, "Please, God, don't let me die here." Going down was either going to cause death or major damage to my person. So the only course of action was to try to go up. After what seemed like an eternity, I was finally able to throw my poles up top along with one of my skis.

Here is where I had to become a human Gumby to make this escape work. Pulling my left ski from the left side of the tree, I grabbed the top of the ski and pushed down in order to leverage my foot in between the tree and the side of the ridge. I caught my breath. Then I took off the ski and used it as an anchor to stab into the snow to drag myself back to the top. As soon as I reached the top, I turned around and just sat there staring down at the rock below.

Within seconds, a guy skied by and asked me, "You okay?" I wanted to say, "Yeah, I am now! Where were you forty-five minutes ago!" Sitting there, reflecting on what had just happened, I looked around, and to my surprise, I noticed that the only tree on the leisure trail, to my left, was the tree that I had been hanging from. For about twenty yards before the tree and thirty yards after the tree, there was nothing that could have stopped me from going straight to the bottom.

I had skied off that mountain at the exact place where there was a tree to catch me. Oh, yeah! So, I begin to think. *How long has this tree been here? When was it planted? Did God strategically place this tree right here knowing that one day Chris Brooks would ski by here, hit a patch of ice, and turn hard left off the side of the mountain?*

Instead of reading about a horrible accident in Colorado, you get to read about how a tree on a mountain saved my life.

It was the tree on which my Lord and Savior was crucified that saved my life, and your life. After gaining my composure, I skied down to the bottom and met up with my buddy, Clyde. "Where have you been?" he asked. What else could I say besides, "Uh, bro, I just skied off the side of the mountain. I've been hanging there for forty-five minutes!" Of course, Clyde said, "We have to go back up so I can see this!"

I remember the tears in Clyde's eyes when he saw the ice and the disturbed snow, not to mention the scrape down the front of the tree from my ski. It looked like a two hundred-pound, twelve-point buck had been there. Then, peering off the side to look down at the bottom, we looked at the creek bed of jagged rocks. Till this day, Clyde and I talk about the Tree of Life in Winter Park, Colorado.

How crazy is it to know that Jesus would be so strategic in every detail of our lives? That's why, when I preach about prayer, I always tell people to be specific in how they pray. I hope that you can see the beautiful picture painted here on the side of this ski resort of the saving Grace of Christ Jesus. You may fall, but if you are a believer, you will never fall past the tree (cross). We always go back to the place where it all began for us. Consider these words from the hymn "Alas! and Did My Savior Bleed," lyrics by Isaac Watts written at the beginning of the eighteenth century:

At the cross, at the cross, where I first saw the light,

And the burden of my heart rolled away,

It was there by faith I received my sight

And now I am happy all the day!

Not to jump ahead, but if Jesus knew that Peter would deny Him three times, then don't you think He would have known that Peter would have the pride issue that we spoke about in the previous chapter? Even though Peter made a mistake when he questioned Jesus about His death, still Jesus was about to invite Peter to go with him to the top of the Mountain of Transfiguration.

God's Mountain

The Bible records that around six days passed between the time of Peter's Satan episode to the episode on the Mountain of Transfiguration. I bet Peter thought he had straight up blown it with Jesus. We don't have a recording of what transpired during those six days. I'm not sure if Peter repented to Jesus. Did they sit down and have a counseling session on how to prevent Satan from using us like puppets? This just proves to me that, even though we may make mistakes, Jesus offers an invitation to take us higher. Matthew 17:1–8 gives us a depiction of what transpired on that mountain:

> Now after six days Jesus took Peter, James, and
> John his brother, led them up on a high mountain
> by themselves; and He was transfigured before
> them. His face shone like the sun, and His clothes
> became as white as the light. And behold, Moses

and Elijah appeared to them, talking with Him. Then Peter answered and said to Jesus, "Lord, it is good for us to be here; if You wish, let us make here three tabernacles: one for You, one for Moses, and one for Elijah." While he was still speaking, behold, a bright cloud overshadowed them; and suddenly a voice came out of the cloud, saying, "This is My beloved Son, in whom I am well pleased. Hear Him!" [6]And when the disciples heard it, they fell on their faces and were greatly afraid. But Jesus came and touched them and said, "Arise, and do not be afraid." When they had lifted up their eyes, they saw no one but Jesus only.

The scripture uses the word *transformed*. I want you, the reader, to understand that Jesus was not transformed into anything. This was the transformation out of the flesh into His true heavenly appearance. Up to this moment, Peter, James, and John had seen Jesus in His earthly body. On this mountaintop experience, they were privy to seeing Jesus in His heavenly form.

This placed absolutely zero doubt in their hearts and minds that He was the Christ—seeing Him in all His brilliance, face shining like the sun, with light protruding from His body. What a remarkable sight that must have been! Also, it must have been amazing to be in a conversation between Jesus, Moses, and Elijah.

I have had the privilege of sitting under some incredible men of God in my life. One of those great men of God taught me that, when you are surrounded by great men of influence, you should do three things: sit down, shut up, and listen! You already know all that you know. Now listen to the wisdom of those with whom you have been given the privilege to sit.

Peter, James, and John sat and listened with amazement to the incredible conversations of this heavenly trifecta. In Luke 9:31, we find out what they were discussing. Jesus discussed what He was about to accomplish at Jerusalem. Jesus then turned His attention to Peter. In verse four, it says, "Then Peter answered and said to Jesus." Mark 9:5 also says, "Peter answered Jesus." Luke gives a different view of Peter just bursting out of nowhere with a statement. Luke 9:33: "Then it happened, as they were parting from Him, that Peter said to Jesus, 'Master, it is good for us to be here; and let us make three tabernacles: one for You, one for Moses, and one for Elijah'—not knowing what he said."

Matthew and Mark both record that Peter answered Jesus. My question is what did Jesus ask Peter? For Peter to answer Jesus, it must mean that Peter was in the conversation and was addressed by Jesus. This is all a matter of speculation and thought process for a moment to get to a very important point.

If Jesus, Moses, and Elijah were speaking about Jesus's death and the cross, then maybe the encounter that Peter and Jesus had six days earlier came up. Maybe Jesus asked Peter, "What do you think about this matter, Peter?" Let's get in Peter's mind for a second. Imagine Peter saying, "Well, you asked me this six days ago, and you rebuked me and called me Satan. That was in front of all the other disciples. Now I'm here with You, Moses, and Elijah, so the pressure is on ten million times right now."

Mark says that they were afraid before the cloud showed up

and they heard a loud voice. "It's good to be here." That makes me laugh! Have you ever done this? I know I have. Not knowing what to say and out comes, "Good to be here." All righty let's see. We got the Son of Man here, the Bearded Wonder, and the passenger in Chariots of Fire. Let's build each one of you a tent to live in, and we can call it Glory Mountain Church. Everybody can come by and visit you guys at Christmas and at Easter.

Even though Peter, James, and John were invited up on the mountain, the question is, can you handle the altitude? I'm reminded of a Scripture, Proverbs 17:28, "Even a fool is counted wise when he holds his peace; When he shuts his lips, he is considered perceptive."

Peter implies, by his response, that Jesus, Moses, and Elijah are equals. Sometimes when I'm reading the Bible I want to say, "Hey, Peter, just shut up, dude! Your life would be a lot easier, man!"

Now, in Matthew 17:5, Peter is about to be rebuked by the Father: "This is My beloved Son, in whom I am well pleased. Hear Him!"

So, can you handle the altitude? Altitude is the high importance of what is coming. Stop and think about this. Peter, being the Rock and the foundation of the church, had a pretty rocky beginning. It was important for Peter to witness what transpired on that mountain.

God may place you on some mountaintops throughout your life. I hope and pray that you will grasp the greater importance of why you are there. It's not to throw around your accolades and degrees. It's not to get attention by name dropping and showing off about all the big-name people that you know. It's about being humble and quiet and thanking God that He chose you to be a part of something awesome!

We get so caught up in what Peter did wrong. How about focusing on the fact that Peter was on the mountain with Jesus and was privileged to see Him in all His glory. Peter will never forget this mountaintop experience, and neither will you.

Seven

Denying Your Call

I love Christmastime. I love the decorations, the trees, and the snow when we have it in the hills of Tennessee. I love getting a cup of coffee and going to look at Christmas lights that are timed to music as they dance across the houses and yards. I especially love watching Christmas movies. My favorite Christmas movies include: *How the Grinch Stole Christmas, Jingle All the Way, A Christmas Story, Home Alone,* and *Home Alone 2: Lost in New York.*

I can't stand any of the Hallmark Christmas shows. It's the same thing over and over: somebody breaks up a long relationship and goes to a small town that's amazing. Then Santa shows up with an elf and there's some pixie dust. Santa throws the magic dust on the girl with the executive job in New York City. Oh, and don't forget that she has a rich boyfriend in New York. Spoiler alert: he will show up later and she will have to choose between money and poverty, even though poverty has six-pack abs. Here's another one: Someone has a dream and works on a farm. A guy shows up because Granny cooked a pie and tells the poor farm boy to give it to the new girl in the small town where everybody

61

loves everybody. Then the twist—the old boyfriend, the girlfriend, the boss, a drunk guy, her absentee dad, and tiny Tim with the wooden leg show up. Oh yeah, and the family dog shows up, but he is really a reindeer. You have about fifteen minutes of unnecessary drama coupled with five thousand commercials. "Dear God, will this ever end so we can watch football? Amen!" Then they all get back together, bake some cookies, and live happily ever after in a small town where everybody loves each other. What's funny is that I can't seem to find that place anywhere on a map of the United States.

I do, however, love all three Santa Clause movies. I laugh so hard all the time at the quick wit of the characters in these movies. In the first movie, *The Santa Clause*, Scott Calvin and his son, Charlie, have an overnight adventure to the North Pole. Afterwards, Scott Calvin has a sit-down with Charlie to discuss the previous night's events. It goes like this:

Scott Calvin: Charlie, I already told ya. We did not go to the North Pole. That was a dream!

Charlie: You're in denial, Dad.

Scott Calvin: You don't even know what that means.

Charlie: Well, you are. I know what happened.

Scott Calvin: How do you know that? How? You don't have any proof.

Charlie: Proof?

Scott Calvin: Why can't we both think of it as just a great dream and forget about it?

Charlie: What about this? Remember all the neat stuff inside?

Scott Calvin: Charlie, this is a toy. We used to make things like this at work, but no one bought 'em. Here. I don't want to talk about this anymore.

Charlie: I know who you are, Dad. You'll figure it out soon enough. There are a lot of kids that believe in you. You can't let them down.

Scott Calvin: Charlie, you're wrong.

"You're in denial." What does it mean to be in denial? According to dictionary.com, denial is "the disbelief in the existence or reality of a thing." While I was a student pastor, I would have to talk with parents about rebellion issues concerning their children. At times I would even have conversations about drug use, and other significant teenage issues. Some parents look at their children as if they are still in diapers, and everything is just fine and going to work itself out. This is called denial.

In Matthew 26 we see several things taking place. Mary breaks open an alabaster box of expensive fragrant oil and pours it on Jesus's head. She also washes his feet with her tears and dries them with her hair, according to John, chapter 12. Judas agrees to betray Jesus. They all celebrate the Passover, and Jesus implements the Lord's Supper. Peter is about to make a strong statement concerning his position with the Lord and his relationship. Matthew 26:31–34:

> When they had sung a hymn, they went out to the Mount of Olives. Then Jesus said to them, "All of you will be made to stumble because of Me this night, for it is written: 'I will strike the Shepherd, And the sheep of the flock will be scattered.' But after I have been raised, I will go before you to Galilee." Peter answered and said to Him, "Even if all are made to stumble because of You, I will never be made to stumble." Jesus said to him, "Assuredly, I say to you that this night, before the rooster crows, you will deny Me three times." Peter said to Him, "Even if I have to die with You, I will not deny You!" And so said all the disciples.

Jesus said that they all would stumble on that night because of Him. We read in *Strong's Exhaustive Concordance of the Bible* that "to stumble" in the Greek is σκανδαλίζω, *skandalizō*, which means "cause to sin or be scattered." We get our word *scandal* from this word. Dictionary.com defines scandal as "a disgraceful or discreditable action, circumstance, an offense caused by a fault or misdeed, damage to reputation; public disgrace, defamatory talk; malicious gossip."

Jesus explains that his disciples would, under the circumstances, be scattered because of what was about to take place. Peter declares that, even if everyone stumbled, he would not: "I will not fall away from you." In John 13 and in Mark 14, Peter makes the same statement. He says that he would die before he left or denied Jesus. Let's look at what the Gospel of Luke says:

And the Lord said, "Simon, Simon! Indeed, Satan has asked for you, that he may sift you as wheat. But I have prayed for you, that your faith should not fail; and when you have returned to Me, strengthen your brethren." But he said to Him, "Lord, I am ready to go with You, both to prison and to death." Then He said, "I tell you, Peter, the rooster shall not crow this day before you will deny three times that you know Me." (Luke 22:31–34)

When the scripture says, "Satan has asked for you," it is literally saying he has demanded your presence. Satan wants to do all he can to get followers of Jesus to tuck tail and run or fail past a point of returning. Satan has demanded to sift you. If we look in *Strong's Exhaustive Concordance of the Bible*, we see that the word *sift* is translated from the Greek word σίναπι *sinapi, sin'-ap-ee;* perh. from σίνομαι sinŏmai (to hurt or to sting); mustard (the plant): —mustard." Literally, he wants to crush you and hurt you, to sting you to the very core.

Jesus says, in Luke 22:32, "But I have prayed for you, that your faith should not fail; and when you have returned to Me, strengthen your brethren." Jesus says He has prayed that our faith will not fail. That's not to say that Satan won't try and crush you. We have seen this in scripture before. Job 1:7–8:

So Satan answered the Lord and said, "From going to and fro on the earth, and from walking back and forth on it." Then the Lord said to Satan, "Have you considered My servant Job, that there is none like him on the earth, a blameless and upright man, one who fears God and shuns evil?"

Satan tells the Lord that the only reason Job loves Him the way that he does is because His hand is on him. Satan tells God that, if He removed his hand from him, then he will curse Him. Job 2:4–6:

So Satan answered the Lord and said, "Skin for skin! Yes, all that a man has he will give for his life. But stretch out Your hand now, and touch his bone and his flesh, and he will surely curse You to Your face!" And the Lord said to Satan, "Behold, he is in your hand, but spare his life."

I can see this happening again with Peter. Satan demands to sift Peter. Jesus prays that Peter will pull through the sifting. However, he does not pray the sifting will not take place. Sometimes I have prayed that the Lord would rebuke the sifting, but what lesson would be learned from always having to be rescued?

Imagine Jesus saying, "I'm praying for you, Peter, praying that your faith won't fail and that, after your walk of denial, you will return to me and strengthen the other disciples." Now, before He entered the garden of Gethsemane, Jesus made a profound statement about the coming conflict that Christians are going to have. Luke 22:35–38:

> And He said to them, "When I sent you without money bag, knapsack, and sandals, did you lack anything?" So, they said, "Nothing." Then He said to them, "But now, he who has a money bag, let him take it, and likewise a knapsack; and he who has no sword, let him sell his garment and buy one. For I say to you that this which is written must still be accomplished in Me: 'And He was numbered with the transgressors.' For the things concerning Me have an end." So they said, "Lord, look, here are two swords." And He said to them, "It is enough."

The time will come when you will need a form of protection because this world is evil. I wanted to bring this up for two reasons. First, I travel around the nation, and I hear people making comments like, "Who needs armed people in the church?" "There is no need." "Are you really walking in faith if you require armed guards?" That's like saying you don't have to lock up your car in public or lock your house at night. Protection is not a fear tactic, it is wisdom.

The second reason is found in Matthew 10:16: "Behold, I send you out as sheep in the midst of wolves. Therefore, be wise as serpents and harmless as doves." Wise, in this case, means to be prepared if a wolf comes by to try and kill the sheep or the shepherd.

Hello! It is going to be very intriguing in the next chapter when we discuss Peter's attempt to kill the high priest's servant.

The Prayer

In Mark 14:32–42, we read:

> Then they came to a place which was named Gethsemane; and He said to His disciples, "Sit here while I pray." And He took Peter, James, and John with Him, and He began to be troubled and deeply distressed. Then He said to them, "My soul is exceedingly sorrowful, even to death. Stay here and watch." He went a little farther, and fell on the ground, and prayed that if it were possible, the hour might pass from Him. And He said, "Abba, Father, all things are possible for You. Take this cup away from Me; nevertheless, not what I will, but what You will." Then He came and found them sleeping, and said to Peter, "Simon, are you sleeping? Could you not watch one hour? Watch and pray, lest you enter into temptation. The spirit indeed is willing, but the flesh is weak." Again He went away and prayed and spoke the same words. And when He returned, He found them asleep again, for their eyes were heavy; and they did not know what to answer Him. Then He came the third time and said to them, "Are you still sleeping and resting? It

is enough! The hour has come; behold, the Son of Man is being betrayed into the hands of sinners. Rise, let us be going. See, My betrayer is at hand."

Jesus asked Peter, James, and John to come alongside Him to watch and pray. The word *watch*, according to *Strong's Exhaustive Concordance of the Bible*, in the Greek is *tereo*, which means "to guard, to be on guard consistently." When Jesus returned to the three after asking His Father if there was another way other than the crucial end he was about to endure, Jesus spoke in the presence of James and John, but He addressed Peter. Little did Peter recognize that this was a sign of leadership.

Jesus was not asking Peter to pray for Him and ask that He would not have to endure the Cross. This beautiful illustration and teaching moment was showing Peter, James, and John how to pray under distress. Not only that, but also how to hear from the Father for direction. Simon could you not watch, stand guard, with me for one hour. Are you asleep!

The sifting of Satan begins with turning hearts away from intercessory prayer and replacing it with a lethargic lifestyle. I can just hear Jesus: "Peter, you are the representation of the church here, now and in times to come! Again, here you are sleeping!" The Christ that he has confirmed with his own lips is asking him to pray with Him for one hour. When He comes to be encouraged by Peter's tenacity, He finds slothfulness.

My hope and prayers are that this compels you to be awakened from being asleep. I pray that it also awakens you to intercession for those around you who are living lethargic lives. The Father is clearly speaking and asking us to stand guard, to watch and pray. Simon, "can you not pray for one hour?"

I spend time in the company of a lot of Pentecostal people and members of charismatic churches. They talk about prayer and past prayer meetings. They talk about how they have been in meetings that lasted for many hours. I myself have been in those prayer meetings. I, for one, make prayer the most important part of my day.

Matthew 6:33 teaches us to seek first the Kingdom, so the first part of every day is spent seeking after the Lord.

Jesus didn't ask Peter to pray for hours. He asked him to pray for one hour. Now you and I both know that, if you pray for one hour, you're going to end up praying longer because of your love and devotion to the Father. If we look deeper into this watching and praying, then we will see that Jesus gave Peter an addendum to the watching and praying. In verse 38, Jesus tells them that if they will watch and pray, then they will avoid temptation.

Matthew 6:9–13:

Our Father in heaven,

Hallowed be Your name.

Your kingdom come.

Your will be done

On earth as it is in heaven.

Give us this day our daily bread.

And forgive us our debts,

As we forgive our debtors.

And do not lead us into temptation,

But deliver us from the evil one.

For Yours is the kingdom and the power and the glory forever. Amen.

In Verse 13, Jesus says, pray "do not lead us into temptation." Deliver us from temptation, of the evil one. This is prayer 101. Pray to the Father that you do not enter into temptation.

In 1 Corinthians 10:13, we read: "No temptation has overtaken you except such as is common to man; but God is faithful, who will not allow you to be tempted beyond what you are able, but with the temptation will also make the way of escape, that you may be able to bear it." With the temptation he will make a way of escape for you.

The Way of Escape

For years I have wondered where the magical push-button escape hatch is. Where is this doorway of escape? How do we achieve it, or find it on a daily basis? The doorway of escape from the dreaded temptations that come our way is opened to us every morning in devotion and prayer. Watch and pray, or you will succumb to the temptation that comes your way. Three times Jesus went to Peter and found them sleeping, fallen to the temptation in their weak flesh. The third time Jesus declared, "Enough!" And His accusers came to take him away. What does your prayer life look like today?

I hear people all the time telling me how they like to pray at night. That's what I used to do for years. What I realized about my nightly prayers is they sounded something like this, "Lord forgive me for what I did, who I did it with, what I said, where I was ..." And this would go on and on and on. The doorway of escape is available to you so that your evening prayers can be more for thanking the Father and loving Him instead of making the dreaded "sorry prayers."

Have you stopped and thanked the Father for all He has done in your life? Have you prayed for one hour today? We are talking about only one hour! Most people spend more than five hours a day watching TV, playing video games, engaging with social media or "stuff" on their phones. Can you not watch and pray for one hour?

What if Jesus came to you right now and said, "I need you. I am vexed to the point of death! Please, put your phone down just for one hour and pray with me. Could you stop what you're doing and pray with me for one hour? I know it's six o'clock in the morning, but would you spend one hour with me praying?" What would you say? What would you do? One hour of watching and prayer will save your life the next time temptation comes your way. It will keep you from making the same habitual mistakes over and over in your life. He's asking you for one hour! Will you stop and pray with Him?

Prayer

Father forgive me for when I have done my own thing and not listened to you when you called me to pray. I am finished with making excuses about why I can't pray in the mornings. I know that, when I pray, you are setting my Spirit up for success when it comes to standing against denial and temptation. I choose today to make prayer a priority in my life. In Jesus's name, Amen

Eight

Forged In Fire

O ne of my favorite television shows to watch is *Forged in Fire* on the History Channel. *Forged in Fire* is a competition between four bladesmiths who have been forging knives for many years. They have anywhere from five years to forty years of experience in making all kinds of knives. There is a panel of judges that critique the overall build of the knives and also puts the blades through a series of tests to see who will be the Forged and Fire champion.

This competition begins in a variety of ways. Each bladesmith stands in front of an anvil. A cloth covers the mystery raw material that is to be used. I have seen ball bearings, motorcycles, Damascus steel, and all kinds of other materials. The materials to be used just make the challenge that much more difficult. Each bladesmith can either make a knife in his or her signature style or a knife according to the style the judges provide.

Even though they can make a knife in their signature style, they still must follow some parameters so that the knife can be used in testing. The cool thing is that the bladesmiths are told what kinds of tests their knives will be performing. The battle begins, and chaos begins immediately. Fire shoots out of the forges while the contestants try to stay calm, all while feeling the heat and the stress of having to build a winning knife in only three hours.

Once the first three hours have elapsed, the knives are evaluated to see if they meet the parameters and to see which knife is the best and which is the worst. Unfortunately, the maker of the worst knife must surrender his or her blade to the judges and then leave the forge. At this time, the competitors are given the next set of instructions. They must fix any irregularities and put fully functioning handles onto their blades. Then they must sharpen their blades for the test.

Next, the knives are put to the test in a few different scenarios. First is the strength test. In this test the judges are not looking for what the blade does to the material it is being tested against, but what happens to the blade. After testing each blade, the judges look for any weaknesses—maybe a broken handle or a rolled or chipped blade. The worst could be a catastrophic failure that breaks the blade into pieces. In this case, the bladesmith is automatically disqualified.

After the strength test is the kill test. Awesome! To spare you any gory details, the blades are tested to see if they can kill. Doug Marcaida says "keeell"—very funny, but all the bladesmiths can't wait for him to say it about their blades. Lastly is the durability test. Can the knife go through all this torture and still be functional enough to continue as a blade? The last two standing win the competition and are sent back to their home forges to make an iconic blade of some sort. After five days, they return and go through the same grueling tests to see who is the Forged and Fire champion!

You may be wondering, "Why all this knife talk?" Here is why: First, Peter was about to be forged in fire in the garden. When Jesus was about to be arrested, an incident took place that we cannot overlook. Now, before I go into our main scripture, let me remind you of some previous scriptures that lead up to this moment. For example, Luke 22:35–38:

> And He said to them, "When I sent you without money bag, knapsack, and sandals, did you lack anything?" So, they said, "Nothing." Then He said to them, "But now, he who has a money bag, let him take it, and likewise a knapsack; and he who has no sword, let him sell his garment and buy one. For I say to you that this which is written must still be accomplished in Me: 'And He was numbered with the transgressors.' For the things concerning Me have an end." So they said, "Lord, look, here are two swords." And He said to them, "It is enough."

Do you have a sword? Jesus asks this question, and the disciples have two swords at the ready. This was such a big deal to Jesus that he told them to sell a garment so they would have money to buy a weapon to have on hand. Two swords among twelve guys. Okay. I would have gone for one per disciple, but that's just me talking. Peter made a remark a few verses earlier: "But he said to Him, 'Lord, I am ready to go with You, both to prison and to death.' Then He said, 'I tell you, Peter, the rooster shall not crow this day before you will deny three times that you know Me'" (Luke 22:33–34).

Peter declares, "I will go to prison with you, or if I have to die, I will die." Now, we are about to get into some good stuff. If you have ever heard me preach, then I say this a lot. So, here I go. Watch this!

> Jesus answered, "I have told you that I am He. Therefore, if you seek Me, let these go their way," that the saying might be fulfilled which He spoke, "Of those whom You gave Me I have lost none." Then Simon Peter, having a sword, drew it and struck the high priest's servant, and cut off his right ear. The servant's name was Malchus. So Jesus said to Peter, "Put your sword into the sheath. Shall I not drink the cup which My Father has given Me?" (John 18:8–11)

Peter drew his sword and swung it at the high priest's servant's head! He wasn't going for his ear; he was going to take his head off! This is Peter we are talking about here. The same guy who had just told Jesus, "I will die for you. You told me to carry a sword, and evil people are coming after us. So, I did what I thought was right, but obviously I was wrong!"

Can you imagine the confusion that must have been running though Peter's mind at this moment? "Do you have a sword?" "Yes." "Good. You're going to need it. You're going to deny me three times, Peter." Standing in front of Malchus, I'm sure Peter was thinking, *I'll show Jesus and all the disciples that I meant what I said, and without thinking this thing through, here I go!* Slice! There goes homeboy's ear flying to the ground.

Jesus stopped Peter. Imagine the conversation! "Put the sword up!" "Wait a minute, Jesus, you said we needed a sword." "Yes! But, I also said that which is written must still be accomplished in Me."

"'And He was numbered with the transgressors.' For the things concerning Me have an end" (Luke 22:37).

How many times have you and I done things in the name of Jesus, thinking that our actions would advance the Kingdom or be of some great benefit only to find out our timing was totally wrong. "Peter, you're going to need this sword after I am arrested and die on the cross. You cannot stop what has to be done here." Jesus said, "Shall I not drink the cup which my Father has given me (John 18:11). "You see, Peter, if you had been watching and praying with me, as I asked you, you would have been privy to what the Father was relaying to me."

Have you ever been so certain about something that, when it didn't happen the way you thought that it should, or it happened in a different time, you took matters into your own hands? Then later you found out that all was being taken care of, and by stepping in to try and make things better you only made matters worse? This is where the Fruit of the Spirit comes into the equation.

In Galatians 5:16–26, we read:

> 1I say then: Walk in the Spirit, and you shall not fulfill the lust of the flesh. For the flesh lusts against the Spirit, and the Spirit against the flesh; and these are contrary to one another, so that you do not do the things that you wish. But if you are led by the Spirit, you are not under the law.

Now the works of the flesh are evident, which are: adultery, fornication, uncleanness, lewdness, idolatry, sorcery, hatred, contentions, jealousies, outbursts of wrath, selfish ambitions, dissensions, heresies, envy, murders, drunkenness, revelries, and the like; of which I tell you beforehand, just as I also told you in time past, that those who practice such things will not inherit the kingdom of God. But the fruit of the Spirit is love, joy, peace, longsuffering, kindness, goodness, faithfulness, gentleness, self-control. Against such there is no law. And those who are Christ's have crucified the flesh with its passions and desires. If we live in the Spirit, let us also walk in the Spirit. Let us not become conceited, provoking one another, envying one another.

Pay close attention to verse 22 for it says that "the *fruit* of the Spirit," not *fruits*. It is one fruit with many moving parts. If you were to cut open a grapefruit, then you would see many triangles. If you take a spoonful of the first triangle, you taste grapefruit. If you take a spoonful of the second triangle, you do not taste apple. This is why to walk in the fruit of the Spirit means that you can't pick and choose which one you want. It's either all nine or none!

Walking in the Spirit means that you walk in all nine fruit. Peter was dealing with some fruit allergies when self-control went out the window in the garden and the sword did the talking. The flesh said, "I will show you who's going to go to prison and die for what I believe in." That stunt could have got Peter crucified right alongside Jesus.

Peter saw what was in front of him. Jesus could see the big picture. Peter saw Jesus about to be taken away. Jesus saw Peter standing outside an upper room declaring the Word of the Lord, and three thousand people getting saved. What are you trying to do this very moment in the name of Jesus? Can you see what is coming, or are you blinded by what's in front of you? Jesus decided to save Peter's life. He picked up Malchus's ear and healed him. This was the last miracle of Jesus, and it saved Peter's life. It also set Peter up for his coming denial.

Think with me for a moment. When was the last time you were so sure of something that you just acted upon it without taking the time to think it through? It could have been an action toward another individual or a counter attack that was supposed to help in the defense of someone you were protecting. Did that person get upset with you for interfering, even though you tried to explain that you were only doing what you thought was right and justifiable?

Whatever the incident was, did it sever your relationship with someone? Do you even talk to that person anymore? Did it drive you to go out on your own? Here we are faced with the daunting task of trying to be right or ask for forgiveness. Whom do you need to forgive right now? Maybe you need to be the bigger person and ask for forgiveness. Whichever it may be, the last thing you want to do is allow one incident to keep you anywhere but in close proximity. Close proximity in relationships is key to growth and intimacy. This is true when it comes to a marriage partner, a spiritual authority, a pastor, and especially when it comes to Jesus.

Nine

Following At A Distance

Hunting squirrels with your dad is just one of those pastimes that good ol' country boys in northeast Texas do on Saturday mornings. I will never forget the first time I went hunting with my dad. Dad was hunting with a pump-action twelve-gauge shotgun, and I had my Papaws single-shot twenty-gauge shotgun. As we traversed through the woods, it was so cold it was almost unbearable. With every breath we could see the vapors hitting the atmosphere.

Every step my dad took was slow and precise. He told me to step where he had stepped so we wouldn't make any excess noise that would scare off the squirrels. The leaves were crunching under our boots, and our eyes were peeled for movement in the trees. I was approximately seven paces behind my dad when he pointed up into the tree in front of us and quietly whispered, "Squirrel." If you have never hunted squirrels before, you won't know just how erratic they can be whether they are in a tree or on the ground. If you have never seen that, then just take my word for it. Squirrels are nuts!

This squirrel took off running across a limb from right to left, I drew my shotgun and pointed in the direction of the squirrel. Before I knew what was happening, I heard a loud bang, to which I responded with a simultaneous bang! At that moment, my dad turned around with eyes as big as saucers! "Boy! You don't shoot behind someone like that! You could have shot *me!*" This would have been great information to have included in our safety briefing before the hunt. Oh yeah, we didn't have a safety briefing!

Sad to say, there was not much left of that squirrel, and I don't remember seeing another that day. What I do remember from that day was what my dad taught me. He said to me, "Don't follow at such a distance. Stay on my heels so I know where you are and we can communicate easier." This means of hunting and warfare was instilled into me by my father and by the United States Army when it came time for me to learn how to shoot, move, and communicate. This was imbedded into my brain. You always know where your battle buddy is, and you never lose eye contact. It's when soldiers so often don't follow these rules that you hear so many cases about friendly fire. It can be caused when you don't know where friendlies are located, especially if they are following at a distance.

Luke 22:54: "Having arrested Him, they led Him and brought Him into the high priest's house. But Peter followed at a distance." I want you to see this scripture in a new fashion after reviewing everything that we have discussed up to this point. Peter was willing to die for Jesus and with Jesus. Peter just didn't understand the greater calling that Jesus had for the Rock. So, we are going to view this scripture based upon modern-day Christianity. The question is this, Do you follow Jesus from a distance? If you do, then the same reactions that Peter experienced could be in your near future.

Let us see what it actually means to follow at a distance. *Strong's Exhaustive Concordance of the Bible* tells us that the Greek word for "follow" is *akoloutheo*, which means "one who precedes with, joins or accompanies." The Greek word for "distance," according to *Strong's Exhaustive Concordance of the Bible*, means "afar off, or from afar." So, when Peter was following Jesus it could be said that Peter pursued Jesus from afar, not to be seen.

Today there are so many people who claim to be Christians but who follow Jesus from a distance. Has Jesus become our get-out-of-jail-free card or our Sunday political self-promotion tool? People use the name of Jesus at sporting events, award ceremonies, on social media, or even from the platforms of churches as their Christian addendum to cover their secret or public lives. I understand that Peter was following at a distance because he wanted to be close to Jesus—just not so close that it would cost him his life. What happens when you live your life from afar?

Luke 22:55–57: "Now when they had kindled a fire in the midst of the courtyard and sat down together, Peter sat among them. And a certain servant girl, seeing him as he sat by the fire, looked intently at him and said, 'This man was also with Him.' But he denied Him, saying, 'Woman, I do not know Him.'"

You may find yourself consumed with man's fire instead of the fire of God. Peter, from afar, decided to take refuge at a fire with the same people who not only hated Jesus, but would soon be screaming, "Crucify Him!"

In 1 Corinthians 15:33, we read, "Do not be deceived: 'Evil company corrupts good habits.'" This is truth that needs to be preached from the pulpits of America! My father-in-law would say, "If you hang around poop, then you're not going to smell like roses!" Living a life halfway is not living.

Revelation 3:15–16 teaches, "I know your works, that you are neither cold nor hot. I could wish you were cold or hot. So then, because you are lukewarm, and neither cold nor hot, I will vomit you out of My mouth."

I can understand someone as passionate as Peter wanting to be close to Jesus. Here we see passion immediately turn to fear and rejection. Peter cries out just a few scriptures earlier, "I will never reject you, Jesus!" Then when he is questioned by one of the crowds in a public manner, "Are you not one of His disciples?" The answer of despair was, "Woman, I don't know Him."

Whose fire are you standing at today? This could be the water cooler at work, the crowds at school in the cafeteria, or the bar after work for a few social drinks before going home. Maybe it is the office of another staff member at church. Fire catches wherever fires are lit. Fire draws people to it. The question is, who's fire are you standing at?

As Peter cozied up to the fire, he listened to the remarks of these people. "He is no prophet! He is a liar! He cast out demons with the power of demons! He is a fraud! He is a fool! He is just a stupid man!" How long are you going to hang out at another man's fire? "Pastor is stupid! Pastor is a fool! Pastor thinks he knows it all!" Sounds like a church I want to attend!

Here is the deal about Peter—he can't run from his attributes.

And a certain servant girl, seeing him as he sat by the fire, looked intently at him and said, "This man was also with Him." You see, something happens once you have lived in the presence—the true presence, not religion. It doesn't matter how hard you try to be something that you're not, you will be found out. You are one of his disciples!

"I recognize you from the church. Don't you go to church? What are you doing at this fire … bar … club … party?" "Woman, I don't know Him!" "I don't go to church! I only go because my parents make me." "My spouse wants me to go. I don't even like it." Weird, huh? This is just how Satan loves to sift believers who are trying to fit into a place of compromise.

Maybe you're playing the fences right now—acting one way on Sunday and returning to the vomit on Monday. Let me be the first to say that this was a habitual characteristic in my own life for a long period of time. You see, you can play the game long enough until finally the game plays you, and you're not even in control any longer. Look at what Paul says about this in Romans 7:15–20:

> For what I am doing, I do not understand. For what I will to do, that I do not practice; but what I hate, that I do. If, then, I do what I will not to do, I agree with the law that it is good. But now, it is no longer I who do it, but sin that dwells in me. For I know that in me (that is, in my flesh) nothing good dwells; for to will is present with me, but how to perform what is good I do not find. For the good that I will to do, I do not do; but the evil I will not

to do, that I practice. Now if I do what I will not to do, it is no longer I who do it, but sin that dwells in me.

One step, one thought, one look, one reaction in the sense of taking the bait that Satan dangles in front of you—this can cause a serious downward spiral. Paul even said that, when he was in the flesh, it was not even him making the decisions anymore, but the flesh making all the calls. For one person, this could be spending money on expensive things to bring satisfaction. To another it could be overeating. For yet another it could be looking at porn on the computer.

One item bought turns into thousands of dollars spent on all sorts of items. One container of ice cream turns into gallons. One image viewed turns in millions. One step away from Jesus, one day not in a place of devotion, and the next thing you know you're in full-blown sin.

In Luke 22:58, we read, "And after a little while another saw him and said, 'You also are of them.' But Peter said, 'Man, I am not!'"

Now, we can see that the longer Peter hung out with the wrong crowd the more violent he became. The first time Peter was approached his response was," Woman, I don't know him." His second response was, "Man, I am not!" You see, Peter's character was changing.

When a believer who was once sold out for Jesus begins to frequently mingle with non-believers, there is a change in the attitude or fruit of the believer. This is not a believer who speaks with non-believers in order to win them to Jesus. This is one who is double dipping from glory to hell. They can become easily irritated when it comes to speaking about Jesus, church, sin, and so forth. The very mention of the name of Jesus could set a person off into a demonic feud. Now before you say, "Wait a minute, Christians can't be possessed by the devil." You would be correct. Although they can be *oppressed* by the devil.

Dictionary.com defines oppression as "to burden with cruel or unjust impositions or restraints; subject to a burdensome or harsh exercise of authority or power: to lie heavily upon (the mind, a person, etc.)." This is exactly what Satan did with Peter when he asked Jesus if he could sift Peter like wheat. If Satan cannot oppress an individual, then he will try and conduce him or her. In this form, the person is not being pressed upon; he or she is being led. A good example of being conduced by the devil is Revelation 2:20: "Nevertheless, I have a few things against you, because you allow that woman Jezebel, who calls herself a prophetess, to teach and seduce My servants to commit sexual immorality and eat things sacrificed to idols."

Jesus was speaking to the corrupt church of Thyatira. We see in *Strong's Exhaustive Concordance of the Bible* that the Greek word for "seduce" is *planao*. Planao means "to lead away from the truth, to lead into error, to deceive, to be led into error, to be led aside from the path of virtue, to go astray, sin, to sever or fall away from the truth." Has something led you away from your relationship with Christ? Is there something or someone leading you away? Maybe it has been so long that you don't even remember what caused you to take the journey you're on right now. Peter has already had two strikes and is up for bat again when this happens. Luke 22:59–60: "Then after about an hour had passed, another confidently affirmed, saying, 'Surely this fellow also was with Him, for he is a Galilean.' But Peter said, 'Man, I do not know what you are saying!'" Matthew 26:74: "Then he began to curse and swear, saying, 'I do not know the Man!'"

Let us consider the timeline of what has occurred here in scripture. We are looking at a matter of two to three hours that have a lapsed. From the time that Peter drew his sword, to this very moment, it has only been about three hours. Can you see that, in a matter of three hours, Satan can take a sold-out passionate man of God and turn him into a vehement creature?

Matthew says that Peter began to curse and swear. He was not using foul language of our time or his time. When Peter began to curse himself he spoke the Greek word *katathematizo* according to *Strong's Exhaustive Concordance of the Bible*, which is the Greek word from the G2596 word *intensive* meaning "to speak down, or against." In *Strong's Exhaustive Concordance of the Bible*, the Greek word for "swear" is *omnyo*, which means "to swear, affirm, promise, threaten, with an oath."

What Peter did in that moment superseded what most people preach. What I have always heard was that Peter began to use cursing language, but what he uttered was way more complex than a few cuss words. Peter said, "I don't care about this man in any way. I don't know Him. I don't believe in Him. As a matter of fact, I swear and promise you with an oath that I have never accepted this man as a part of my life!" Peter swore with an oath cursing the day of his encounter with Jesus. Luke 22:60–62: "Immediately, while he was still speaking, the rooster crowed. And the Lord turned and looked at Peter. Then Peter remembered the word of the Lord, how He had said to him, 'Before the rooster crows, you will deny Me three times.' So Peter went out and wept bitterly."

Peter, this is what you swore against: the cleansing of lepers, healing a centurion's daughter, healing your mother-in-law, healing the sick, calming the storm, casting out demons into a herd of swine, healing a paralytic, raising a ruler's daughter, healing a woman with a twelve-year issue of blood, healing two blind men, casting a demon out of a mute man, healing a man's withered hand, feeding five thousand, walking on water, feeding four thousand, healing a gentile woman's daughter, healing an epileptic boy, paying the temple tax with money from a fish's mouth, witnessing a fig tree wither, healing a deaf mute, healing a paralytic, escaping from a hostile mob, watching fish appear in a net dropped off the side of the boat, loosing a bent-over woman, healing a man with dropsy, restoring Malchus's ear, turning water into wine, and raising Lazarus. Not to mention all the teachings, prayers, and parables. You swore against your seat in the heavenly places.

When we deny the Lord, in any fashion, that denial manifests itself outwardly in so many different ways. The first area of compromise is in the exchange of fires. Peter walked with the light when he walked with Jesus. He had a supernatural fire that was imparted unto him by the authority of Christ, according to Matthew Chapter 10. When Jesus gave the disciples this authority, he didn't take it back. I firmly believe that the Holy Spirit has given the church all the abundance of authority and power that Jesus had on the earth.

Unfortunately, instead of receiving this power by faith and administering it to a sleeping church and a dying world, so many are standing around with their hands in their pockets waiting for Jesus to show up and do the work of the Gospel for them. Hear me clearly, beloved, Jesus has already done all He is going to do until the day He is sent back here by the Father. Therefore, He gave you and me His Holy Spirit to continue the love of Christ on this earth.

Additionally, people exchange fires when Jesus is no longer enough. I have heard people say, "Well, I used to pray in the Spirit, I used to lay hands on the sick, I used to do those things, but the fire went out." "I was on fire at the conference, and when I left the conference things were good for about two weeks, but then the fire just went out." How can an eternal flame just go out?

Did we experience the same fire that Moses experienced? Moses had an incredible encounter with the burning bush in the presence of the Lord. After Moses left the burning bush, we no longer hear about a bush burning out in the wilderness. No. We hear about the man Moses burning with the intensity of the Lord. What was on the bush was transferred to the man.

I can guarantee that the reason that the fire of excitement goes out after a conference is the product of no prayer and no Word. The less you pray, the less you read, the less time you spend in the presence of the Father (Hello, fire!), and the less you walk in that fire. Then, you go looking for a fire substitute. Only you know what your fire substitute is. It is whatever draws you away from His presence.

One day you're sitting in church with hands raised high, glorifying God. The next day you're sitting around with people degrading the name of Jesus and anything that is affiliated with Him. It can be as easy as wanting to just take a day off form spending time with Jesus. Don't even, for one second, think that Satan has stopped watching and waiting in the shadows for you to take one step in the wrong direction.

The intensity of your fire is not determined by Sunday morning services. We need to understand something about fire. Fire must be fed in order for there to be heat. Without a source of fuel, the fire will burn out. One source of fuel here on the earth is wood. The more wood you add to the fire, the longer the fire will burn, and the hotter the flame will be. In a spiritual sense, the flame of God will never burn out, although the flame of God can burn out inside of you if you decide to quit feeding the fire.

The flame of your fire is not based on the next revival meeting, conference, or weekly service. Your fire, and the intensity of that fire, is determined by how close you are to the Son. Don't tell me that you're dry either! That's awesome! Dry stuff can catch on fire quicker than wet stuff! Holy Spirit is calling you back to presence, to embrace His fire.

If we continue down the road of hanging out at man's fire, then the next area of concern becomes our identity. When Peter denied Jesus, he did not just deny Jesus; he also denied Petros. Peter was saying, "I curse the day that Jesus transformed my old identity and made me a new man." This is the denial of the blessing he spoke over you, the new identity he gave you as someone with a destiny and a purpose.

With every passing day, you begin to forget who Jesus proclaimed you to be. Isn't it crazy how the mind works in tearing the Spirit person from the flesh person? Your thoughts begin to change. You don't think the way you used to think. You can't even remember scripture. The enemy wants to rob you of your identity. Satan doesn't want you to quote scriptures over yourself. He wants you to feel down and dirty, condemned, broken, with no purpose. He wants you to forget the past experiences of miracles, signs, and wonders. "I can do this on my own! I can figure this out on my own!" You say this until you can't recognize your face in the mirror.

You may find yourself, right here, in this very moment, in the same situation that Peter was facing. Your life is not over! Don't listen to the enemy telling you that you can't bounce back from this horrible incident. Satan will use as many expletives as he can come up with to get you to stay in a place of misery. Hold on tight! Your restoration is on its way!

Ten

Identity Restored

I was sitting in my office, staring out the window, looking at the clouds go by, wondering, *What am I doing here? I need to get out of here now!* Some people would look from the outside, and say, "Wow, Chris has it all going for him—working in a mega church with a large student ministry and awesome leaders. His church is on TV, and he's running a huge student conference. Man, I wish I had that life!" Be careful what you ask for.

I can remember that day as if it was yesterday. My thoughts were running out of control. I felt schizophrenic as my mind was bombarded with thoughts of lust, suicide, anger, frustration, and confusion. I had just had a terrible phone conversation with someone whom I thought was very close to me and had my best interests at heart.

I kept hearing voices in my head saying, "Get out of here now! Go before it's too late!" I began to reflect upon my old job as a chemical engineer for Halliburton. I even tried to contact them to see if I could get my old job back. Funny how I never heard back from anyone. I began to look up MonsterJobs.com, thinking

Maybe I'm not supposed to be in the ministry. (Side note: This is why you need true spiritual fathers and mothers, and Kingdom relationships to keep you on track and focus.)

I have said this before, and I will say it until the day that I die: church staff members should function as a family not an organization. We can lose our focus with daily business, emails, phone calls, and details while thinking we are advancing the Kingdom. In reality, we can be actually sinking deeper into a black hole of empty results. I stood up from my desk, gathered by belongings, and walked out the door.

I spoke to my wife, Davi, on the way out, and said, "I'm going for a drive." I drove out to a nearby lake, parked my truck near the water, and just sat there for hours. During this time, I grabbed my Glock 43 and sat it in my lap. All I could do was try to talk myself out of just ending it all and pulling the trigger. *I can make it all be over in a second! The pain will be gone! What do I have to live for? I'm not even a good preacher! I have no anointing! I have nothing to say to the body of any significance!*

Over and over, the bombardment of satanic conversations filled my head. I truly, in that moment, understood what Jesus went through in the wilderness. Except I wasn't responding with the Word; instead, I was responding with fear and anxiety. My phone rang constantly while I sat there staring into the abyss. After about five hours, I answered a call from my wife, Davi. "I can't take it anymore!" I told her.

A close friend of mine called. He tried his hardest to encourage me and asked if he could come and sit with me. I wanted no part of any person around me. This was a battle that was living inside me. In my stupidity, I was trying to work things out for myself instead of inviting help in the form of good godly advice. Then, all of a sudden, something came into my truck like a wind.

I remember it blew from left to right through my rolled-down windows. I heard the Lord say, "You're miserable, Chris, because you're not walking in the calling in which I called you." At first, I didn't clearly understand what I had just heard. What I had been doing for the past fifteen years had to have been what God was directing me to do. I mean, you get called into the ministry. Then, you pick a field that best suits your gifts. You go into that field and begin to work. Not so!

I had been driving every day to a job instead of resting in my calling. I can clearly say that there is nothing worse than waking up every day and hating the fact that you are about to spend eight hours of your life someplace when, all the while, you are wishing upon a star that you could be somewhere else. I can, with a clear conscience, say that this is an epidemic in this world that causes 95 percent of adult suicide, divorce, and stress. I mean, there were plaques on the wall, ordinations, a college degree, and I was miserable.

I have seen too many people try to treat the symptom more than the issue. When you lose your identity it's easy for the enemy to creep into your life. Fear, doubt, confusion, depression, to name a few, can be the driving factor of an identity crisis. I remember a day when I had prophesied a word from the Lord during one of our services. Later I found out how people were having meetings and gossiping about me, and the prophetic word. This confusion and doubt filled situation shut up the gifts in me for a long time.

It also drove me to listen more to the enemy that shouted, *"You can't preach! You have no Word! Your prophetic edge is a joke!"* This situation is just one avenue is which Satan himself will try and steal your identity. This is why it is vitally important to know who the Lord is and who He says you are!

I am eternally grateful for my wife Davi. She prayed for me, stood by my side, all the while confirming in me who the Lord said that I was, rather than the enemy. I am also thankful for the men of God in my life that had such an integral part in this season. During these spiritually eye-opening meetings with my pastor and Spiritual Father, the entire focus was on restoring my true identity. Some would ask, "How do you stop the voices of distraction in your mind?" My reply is and always will be, "Only by the Holy Spirit!" With the leading of Holy Spirit, my focus was on my identity more than my situation.

My dad once told me that, if I chose to do whatever I loved to do, then I wouldn't work a day in my life. That's what I wanted! I wanted to wake up in the morning with purpose and drive, knowing that I was facing a day that the Lord had made for Chris to conquer. I wanted to be excited about what God had in store for me and my family.

In Ephesians 4:1–6, we read:

> I, therefore, the prisoner of the Lord, beseech you to walk worthy of the calling with which you were called, with all lowliness and gentleness, with longsuffering, bearing with one another in love, endeavoring to keep the unity of the Spirit in the

bond of peace. There is one body and one Spirit, just as you were called in one hope of your calling; one Lord, one faith, one baptism; one God and Father of all, who is above all, and through all, and in you all.

Paul is giving us a common courtesy to make sure we are walking a worthy path and living life encompassed in the specific calling in which Jesus called us. I have made it an enormous factor in my ministry not to speak anything into someone's life that has not already been confirmed by the Holy Spirit. How do I do that? I ask them, "Is what I am saying to you making any sense?" If it's not, I stop! If it is, then I continue to release the discernment of spirits that brings revelation and knowledge to the believer. This brings confirmation that God knows right where that person is and what he or she is going through.

I was called by God, not by man, to pursue Kingdom ministry. Yes, at the time I was in a denomination. Now I speak in a lot of different circles. Therein lies the challenge. When I said yes to Jesus, everything began to come into alignment. Your yes is what the Lord is patiently waiting for. Confusion sets in when we allow others to determine the direction of our lives instead of listening to Holy Spirit.

The Kingdom is not a step ladder to success in ministry. Starting at what some have called the bottom tier of ministry and then working your way to a senior pastor position is not the objective. Here is an example of how distorted this directional endangerment has become: An individual answers an altar call at church, camp, or a conference. Somewhere after that, the individual is told by a staff member, or outside source, that they believe he or she is called to the mission field, evangelism, children's ministry, students' ministry, or other ministry.

Instead, this new believer should be directed on a path to intimacy in prayer and the Word. Unfortunately, in some of our more prophetic circles, some have tried to be God with directional information instead of teaching the believer to have an ear to hear. Rather, new believers should be instructed like this: "Now that you have heard from the Lord, go and seek His face on whichever part of the fivefold you have been molded for. Once you have heard the answer, you can then walk worthy of the calling in which you were called from the beginning of time."

We must quit telling people they are called to the ministry that has a hole in the bucket in order to fill a gap in their own ministry mess! Let the Lord speak to them so that they can walk in peace, and let the measure of anointing be given to accomplish what the Lord declares. After the rooster crowed, and Peter took off weeping, Jesus was crucified on the cross at Calvary. I'm sure some crazy thoughts were firing off in Peter's mind.

Imagine Peter thinking, *Look at all the years you have wasted with this guy! He is dead and not coming back! These crazy women think they saw him outside the tomb! Some of my brothers even said they saw him! He's dead! He's not coming back! All I have done is waste three years of my life! Why don't I just go back and be a fisherman again!*

We read in John 21:1–3:

> After these things Jesus showed Himself again to
> the disciples at the Sea of Tiberias, and in this way
> He showed Himself: Simon Peter, Thomas called
> the Twin, Nathanael of Cana in Galilee, the sons
> of Zebedee, and two others of His disciples were
> together. Simon Peter said to them, "I am going
> fishing." They said to him, "We are going with you
> also." They went out and immediately got into the
> boat, and that night they caught nothing.

Can I just tell you how much Jesus loves you? You see, when
I tried to leave the church and go back to Halliburton, no one
there returned my calls. Now, most people would view that as,
"Keep searching until you find another number. Then call and
call again." Not for me. That was the love of the Father letting me
know that Halliburton was not the answer for my life. I want to
bless you with this: I pray and declare over you today that if you
ever try to go back to the old man and pick up where you left off,
then you will be a huge failure!

You may say, "Wow! I can't believe you just prophesied that people would be failures!" Yes, I did! Here is why. God will not let you succeed in a profession that He has not called you to be successful in. Neither will he let you succeed in your old flesh. Now, you may be successful in the job you are doing while you are on your way to where God is trying to position you. I was very successful at Halliburton, but that was a step in the direction that the Lord had planned for me.

My experiences during the time I worked at Halliburton were nothing more than the Holy Spirit showing me just how faithful God was in my life. Although I once tried to go back to being that old guy, I would not try it again today. Watch this! These guys were professional fisherman. I mean, we're talking about the Bill Dance of biblical times, y'all. They fished all night and caught nothing! If they had caught a bunch of fish, then we might have seen someone else standing in the upper room on the Day of Pentecost.

Remember what I said: God will not let you be successful if you go back to your old ways. Before I get to what happens next, I want to take you on short detour. Let's go back to the day that Peter encountered Jesus. Jesus told Peter to follow him; Jesus would make Peter a fisher of men. "Men," in this case, represents male and female souls on the earth. Matthew tells us that the fishermen left their nets and followed Jesus. Well, they didn't just leave the nets. They also left the boats.

Having read John chapter 21, we know that they remembered where they left those boats tied up. In retrospect, Peter had tied his boat up to the dock three years earlier, after his encounter with Jesus. Leaving it there was his plan B: "If this whole Jesus, fisher-of-men thing doesn't work out, then at least I know where my boat is." I would have thought that Peter would of known the story of Elijah and Elisha.

In 1 Kings 19:19–21 we read:

> So he departed from there, and found Elisha the son of Shaphat, who was plowing with twelve yoke of oxen before him, and he was with the twelfth. Then Elijah passed by him and threw his mantle on him. And he left the oxen and ran after Elijah, and said, "Please let me kiss my father and my mother, and then I will follow you." And he said to him, "Go back again, for what have I done to you?" So Elisha turned back from him, and took a yoke of oxen and slaughtered them and boiled their flesh, using the oxen's equipment, and gave it to the people, and they ate. Then he arose and followed Elijah, and became his servant.

Elisha's yoke of oxen and his plow were his livelihood, his means of accruing finances, which his family used for living expenses and for trading goods. Elisha did something remarkable. He took what had been given to him—his plow equipment—dismantled it, and built an altar. He then sacrificed his oxen, boiled the meat, and gave it to his people to eat. Why did he do this in front of his people? Once Elijah's mantle brushed up against Elisha, he made his mind up that his days of being behind the plow were over!

Dismantling the yoke, sacrificing the oxen, and feeding their meat to his people, was a symbolic gesture meant to show that Elisha was now on a new path and was not going to return to the old one. All who ate of Elisha's oxen knew he was never going back to plow the field ever again, but he was going to follow his calling in a field designed by God.

After Peter had his encounter with Jesus, he should have drilled a hole in that boat and sunk it to the bottom of the sea, ensuring that there was absolutely nothing of that old life to return too. What do you need to dismantle in your life to follow the mantle that God has intended for you to carry?

Jesus Shows Up

In John 21:4–14, we read:

> But when the morning had now come, Jesus stood on the shore; yet the disciples did not know that it was Jesus. Then Jesus said to them, "Children, have you any food?" They answered Him, "No." And He said to them, "Cast the net on the right side of the boat, and you will find some." So, they cast, and now they were not able to draw it in because of the multitude of fish. Therefore that disciple whom Jesus loved said to Peter, "It is the Lord!" Now when Simon Peter heard that it was the Lord, he put on his outer garment (for he had removed it) and plunged into the sea. But the other disciples came in the little boat (for they were not far from land,

but about two hundred cubits), dragging the net with fish. Then, as soon as they had come to land, they saw a fire of coals there, and fish laid on it, and bread. Jesus said to them, "Bring some of the fish which you have just caught." Simon Peter went up and dragged the net to land, full of large fish, one hundred and fifty-three; and although there were so many, the net was not broken. Jesus said to them, "Come and eat breakfast." Yet none of the disciples dared ask Him, "Who are You?"—knowing that it was the Lord. Jesus then came and took the bread and gave it to them, and likewise the fish. This is now the third time Jesus showed Himself to His disciples after He was raised from the dead.

I Love the way Jesus used the same aspect of redemption for Peter, from the same encounter that set Peter in right alignment. When Peter dropped that net off the side of the boat and pulled it up full of fish, his mind sprinted back to the day that he met Jesus: "Wait a minute! I have been here before! That's Jesus!" As zealous as Peter was, he jumped into the water and began to swim to Jesus. I find it amusing that the scripture lets us know that Peter and the boat made it to shore at the same time. Patience can keep you dry! I find it ironic that this was the third time that Jesus showed himself to His disciples, and the first time He addressed Peter. Peter denied his relationship with Jesus three times, and Jesus was about to restore Peter with three questions. John 21:15–19:

So when they had eaten breakfast, Jesus said to Simon Peter, "Simon, son of Jonah, do you love Me more than these?" He said to Him, "Yes, Lord; You know that I love You." He said to him, "Feed My lambs." He said to him again a second time, "Simon, son of Jonah, do you love Me?" He said to Him, "Yes, Lord; You know that I love You." He said to him, "Tend My sheep." He said to him the third time, "Simon, son of Jonah, do you love Me?" Peter was grieved because He said to him the third time, "Do you love Me?" And he said to Him, "Lord, You know all things; You know that I love You." Jesus said to him, "Feed My sheep. Most assuredly, I say to you, when you were younger, you girded yourself and walked where you wished; but when you are old, you will stretch out your hands, and another will gird you and carry you where you do not wish." This He spoke, signifying by what death he would glorify God. And when He had spoken this, He said to him, "Follow Me."

Jesus always address Peter as Simon except in Luke 22:34. Let's go back for just a moment of refreshing. In Chapter 4, Transformation, we learned that Jesus confirmed Simon and gave him the new name of Peter, meaning the Rock. So, to find out what the name Simon means, we need to do some digging and some really quick research. To understand the background of a Jew like Simon, and the origin of his name, we can't look into the Greek translation. We need to go to the Hebrew. According to *Strong's Exhaustive Concordance of the Bible*: Σίμων Simōn, "see'-mone; of Heb. or. [8095]; Simon (i.e. Shimon), the name of nine Isr.: —Simon." Here is the Hebrew translation of Simon: "Shim'ôwn, shim-ōne'; from 8085; hearing; Shimon, one of Jacob's sons, also the tribe desc. from him: —Simeon."

Simon means "hearing." This makes sense when we learn that Jesus addressed Simon and said to him "Blessed are you, Simon Bar-Jonah, for flesh and blood has not revealed this to you, but My Father who is in heaven" (Matthew 16:17).

So, we know that Peter has ears to hear what the Father is saying. Let's go a step further into the root word of his name: "Shâma', shaw-mah'; a prim. root; to hear intelligently (often with impl. of attention, obedience, etc.; caus. to tell, etc.):—× attentively, call (gather) together, × carefully, × certainly, consent, consider, be content, declare, × diligently, discern, give ear, (cause to, let, make to) hear (-ken, tell), × indeed, listen, make (a) noise, (be) obedient, obey, perceive, (make a) proclamation), publish, regard, report, shew (forth), (make a) sound, × surely, tell, understand, whosoever [heareth], witness."

Peter is not just a hearer of the Word; he has the mental capacity to hear intelligently, pay attention, and be obedient to the Word, which is Jesus. I believe that, when Jesus is addressing Simon by name, He is addressing his old nature—not the hearing nature, but the flesh nature. Why else would the Lord give him the new identity of an intellectual, steadfast, hearing church? This is why it is imperative that our hearing be fine-tuned to the voice of Holy Spirit.

Before Simon could completely live the rest of his life as Petros, he had to be restored back to his God-called identity. Three times Peter denied Jesus, and three times Jesus asked Peter if he loved Him. Each time Jesus asked Peter if he loved him, he was killing the "old man" and renewing the "Spirit man." "Do you love me, Simon?" "Do you love me with a supreme (agapao) love?" Peter answered, "Yes, I like you as a friend (*phileo*)."

"Take care of my sheep. Give them the word that I have given you! Simon, are you sure you love me?" "Yes, I like you a lot." "Then, be a shepherd to my people. Simon, do you like me as your friend?" This grieved Peter because Jesus flipped the script on him and asked in the response that Peter had been giving. This humbled Peter, and he answered with, "You know all things. You know I love you as my friend."

Peter denied three times; Jesus restored Peter three times. This was needed in preparation for what was coming. Now some would wonder why Peter did not answer Jesus with agapao love. This is the Love of God. I'm not sure we will be able to fully comprehend this type of love until we are in Heaven. So, understand that the phileo love that Peter had for Jesus was not a bad thing. I have heard this preached as a slap across the face to Jesus. Not so!

This is a conversation between two best friends. Jesus made it plain, "If you are my friend, then you are not my enemy." Peter's response was a heartfelt repentance that he would never curse their relationship ever again. Whomever came around Peter from that day forward would know that Peter was a friend of Jesus.

Maybe you have found yourself in this same predicament that Peter was caught up in. Maybe you have declared some things you wish you had never said. Well, it's just as easy for you to have your restoration moment with Jesus as it was for Peter. I don't believe there is one perfect prayer out there, except for the Lord's Prayer in Matthew 6.

All you must do is humble yourself right now as Peter did at the side of the sea as he sat with others around a fire eating some fish. Allow the wind of God to blow into your situation the way He did into my truck. If you do, then wherever you are, you can make this declaration and decree over your life right now:

> Jesus, your Word says that if I will confess my sins, then you are faithful and just to forgive me. You will cleanse me from all unrighteousness. I confess that I have made vows, cursed, and said that I don't know you. I renounce those statements now and ask for forgiveness. I accept you as my Lord, my Savior, and my Friend. As you restored Peter from his old nature, I receive the same restoration in my life and in our relationship. I thank you for hearing me pray and accepting my request. In Jesus's name, I love you. Amen

References

Dake, Finis. *Dake's Annotated Reference Bible: The Holy Bible, Containing the Old and New Testaments of the Authorized or King James Version Text.* Lawrenceville, Georgia: Dake Publishing, Inc., 2014.

Strong, James. *Strong's Exhaustive Concordance of the Bible.* Peabody, Massachusetts: Hendrickson Publisher, 2007.

Chris Brooks Ministries

www.chrisbrooksministries.com

Christ is our message! We preach to awaken hearts
and bring every person into the full understanding
of truth. It has become my inspiration and passion in
ministry to labor with a tireless intensity, with His power
flowing through me, to present to every believer the
revelation of being His perfect one in Jesus Christ."
Colossians 1:28-29 (The Passion Translation)

Our Mission:

To see the church come back into its full purpose. We have a
passion to harvest and provoke believers to grow on a deeper,
more intimate level with Christ. Through conferences, camps,
discipleship, and connecting with churches, we desperately want
to see people of all ages experience a life changing encounter with
God that will produce consistency and commitment for lasting
revival, both personally and corporately.

To partner in this kingdom work and invest into seeing lives changed for His glory, invite Chris to your next event, and for so much more, visit our website www.chrisbrooksministries.com for details.

Facebook - @chrisbrooksministries
Instagram - @chrisbrooksministries
Twitter -@ChrisBrooksMin
YouTube: Chris Brooks Ministries
Email - info@chrisbrooksministries.com

About the Author

Chris Brooks is a follower of Jesus, husband, father, friend, mentor, and an example to all of what it is like to be a genuine Man of God. He was born in Longview Texas, graduated from Henderson High School, attended Kilgore Jr college before deciding to enlist in the United States Army. Chris served 6 years on active duty, serving around the world. He achieved the rank of Sergeant along with priceless leadership qualities that was preparing him for the life called to advance the kingdom. After leaving the Military Chris was a Chemical Engineer for Halliburton for three years, all the while the Lord was grooming him for ministry. He and his wife, Davi, have been in full time ministry since 2001. While serving at two large church's Chris obtained a Bachelor of Science Degree in Biblical Studies. Signs, wonders, and miracles have been a norm and fruitful evidence of their time advancing the Kingdom of God. January 2017, they started the journey of full-time evangelism. Since their full-time travel schedule in 2017, Chris and Davi have developed a culture of revival at each assignment they encountered. Through long lasting relationships with the church communities that Chris imparts into, they are able to help the local Pastor shift their communities into a place where a revival lifestyle has become the norm. His reach is beyond the four walls of the church using the different forms of social media platforms, worldwide. Through his raw, down to earth, easily understandable communication style, Chris reaches male and female audiences, as well as all ages, equally as effectively. His sense of humor and wealth of insight in to the word of God brings joy, encouragement, and excitement coupled with empowerment that will drive you to embrace the "you" God created you to be.

Chris currently lives in the Chattanooga, Tn area with his wife - Davi and daughter - Faith, who is attending Ministry College at their Home Church Redemption to the Nations.